JO KATHY

BEST,

HAMLET

Hamlet

and Related Readings

McDougal Littell
A HOUGHTON MIFFLIN COMPANY

Evanston, Illinois   *Boston*   *Dallas*

Acknowledgments

Addison-Wesley Educational Publishers Inc.: Excerpt from *The Complete Works of Shakespeare*, 4th edition, by David Bevington. Copyright © 1992 by HarperCollins Publishers Inc. Reprinted by permission of Addison-Wesley Educational Publishers Inc.

W. W. Norton & Company, Inc.: "Father and Son," from *The Poems of Stanley Kunitz 1928–1978* by Stanley Kunitz. Copyright 1944 by Stanley Kunitz. Reprinted by permission of W. W. Norton & Company, Inc.

The University of Chicago Press: "Ophelia" by Arthur Rimbaud, from *Rimbaud: Complete Works, Selected Letters*, translated and edited by Wallace Fowlie. Copyright © 1966 by The University of Chicago. All rights reserved. Reprinted by permission of The University of Chicago Press.

Grove/Atlantic, Inc.: "The Management of Grief," from *The Middleman and Other Stories* by Bharati Mukherjee. Copyright © 1988 by Bharati Mukherjee. Used by permission of Grove/Atlantic, Inc.

University of Texas Press: "Tell Them Not to Kill Me!" from *The Burning Plain and Other Stories* by Juan Rulfo, translated by George D. Schade. Copyright © 1953, translation copyright © 1967, renewed 1996. Reprinted by permission of the University of Texas Press.

Continued on page 350.

Cover illustration by John Kleber.
Author image: North Wind Picture Archives

ISBN 0-395-77554-X

56789—QNT—00   99

Contents

The Tragedy of Hamlet, Prince of Denmark

William Shakespeare

Characters

The Ghost

Hamlet, Prince of Denmark, son of the late King Hamlet and Queen Gertrude

Queen Gertrude, widow of King Hamlet, now married to Claudius

King Claudius, brother to the late King Hamlet

Ophelia

Laertes, her brother

Polonius, father of Ophelia and Laertes, councillor to King Claudius

Reynaldo, servant to Polonius

Horatio, Hamlet's friend and confidant

COURTIERS AT THE DANISH COURT

Voltemand

Cornelius

Rosencrantz

Guildenstern

Osric

Gentlemen

A Lord

DANISH SOLDIERS

Francisco

Barnardo

Marcellus

Fortinbras, Prince of Norway

A Captain in Fortinbras's army

Ambassadors to Denmark from England

Players who take the roles of Prologue, Player King, Player Queen, and Lucianus in *The Murder of Gonzago*

Two Messengers

Sailors

Gravedigger

Gravedigger's companion

Doctor of Divinity

Attendants, Lords, Guards, Musicians, Laertes's Followers, Soldiers, Officers

Place: Denmark

2 **unfold yourself:** show who you are.

ACT ONE

Scene 1 *A guard platform at Elsinore Castle.*

The play opens on the castle walls, where Horatio has joined two soldiers who claim to have seen a spirit. Horatio doubts their story, but when the Ghost appears he agrees that it resembles the recently deceased King of Denmark. Twice he tries unsuccessfully to speak with the Ghost. After it vanishes a second time, Horatio says he will describe what they have seen to Prince Hamlet, son of the late king.

[*Enter* Barnardo *and* Francisco, *two sentinels.*]

Barnardo. Who's there?

Francisco. Nay, answer me. Stand and unfold yourself.

Barnardo. Long live the King!

Francisco. Barnardo.

5   **Barnardo.** He.

Francisco. You come most carefully upon your hour.

Barnardo. 'Tis now struck twelve. Get thee to bed, Francisco.

Francisco. For this relief much thanks. 'Tis bitter cold, And I am sick at heart.

10   **Barnardo.** Have you had quiet guard?

Francisco. Not a mouse stirring.

Barnardo. Well, good night.
    If you do meet Horatio and Marcellus,

14 *rivals of my watch:* the other soldiers on guard duty with me.

16–17 Horatio and Marcellus identify themselves as friendly to Denmark (*this ground*) and loyal subjects of the Danish king (*the Dane*).

27–33 Marcellus explains that Horatio doubts their story about having twice seen a ghost (*apparition*), so he has brought Horatio to confirm what they saw (*approve our eyes*).

The rivals of my watch, bid them make haste.

[*Enter* Horatio *and* Marcellus.]

15 **Francisco.** I think I hear them.—Stand ho! Who is there?

Horatio. Friends to this ground.

Marcellus. And liegemen to the Dane.

Francisco. Give you good night.

Marcellus. O farewell, honest soldier. Who hath
relieved you?

20 **Francisco.** Barnardo hath my place. Give you good night.

[Francisco *exits.*]

Marcellus. Holla, Barnardo.

Barnardo. Say, what, is Horatio there?

Horatio. A piece of him.

Barnardo. Welcome, Horatio.—Welcome, good
Marcellus.

25 **Horatio.** What, has this thing appeared again tonight?

Barnardo. I have seen nothing.

Marcellus. Horatio says 'tis but our fantasy
And will not let belief take hold of him
Touching this dreaded sight twice seen of us.
30 Therefore I have entreated him along
With us to watch the minutes of this night,
That, if again this apparition come,
He may approve our eyes and speak to it.

Horatio. Tush, tush, 'twill not appear.

Barnardo.   Sit down awhile,
35 And let us once again assail your ears,
That are so fortified against our story,
What we have two nights seen.

40 *star . . . pole:* the North Star.

41 *his:* its.

46–50 It was commonly believed that a ghost could only speak after it was spoken to, preferably by someone learned enough (*a scholar*) to ask the proper questions.

48 *harrows:* torments.

50 *usurp'st:* unlawfully takes over.

52 *majesty of buried Denmark:* the buried King of Denmark.

53 *sometimes:* formerly.

Horatio.   Well, sit we down,
  And let us hear Barnardo speak of this.

Barnardo. Last night of all,
40 When yond same star that's westward from the pole
  Had made his course t' illume that part of heaven
  Where now it burns, Marcellus and myself,
  The bell then beating one—

[*Enter* Ghost.]

Marcellus. Peace, break thee off! Look where it comes
  again.

45 **Barnardo.** In the same figure like the King that's dead.

Marcellus [*to* Horatio]. Thou art a scholar. Speak to it,
  Horatio.

Barnardo. Looks he not like the King? Mark it, Horatio.

Horatio. Most like. It harrows me with fear and wonder.

Barnardo. It would be spoke to.

Marcellus.   Speak to it, Horatio.

50 **Horatio.** What art thou that usurp'st this time of night,
  Together with that fair and warlike form
  In which the majesty of buried Denmark
  Did sometimes march? By heaven, I charge thee,
    speak.

Marcellus. It is offended.

Barnardo.   See, it stalks away.

55 **Horatio.** Stay! speak! speak! I charge thee, speak!

[Ghost *exits.*]

Marcellus. 'Tis gone and will not answer.

Barnardo. How now, Horatio, you tremble and look
  pale.
  Is not this something more than fantasy?

61–62 ***Without . . . eyes:*** without seeing the proof (***avouch***) with my own eyes. *Does Horatio seem to be a trustworthy witness? What clues in this scene would support your answer?*

65 ***Norway:*** the King of Norway.

66 ***parle:*** parley, meeting with an enemy.

67 ***smote:*** defeated; ***sledded Polacks:*** Polish soldiers riding in sleds.

69 ***jump:*** exactly.

71–73 Horatio isn't sure what to make of this encounter, but he feels that it is a bad omen (***bodes some strange eruption***) for Denmark.

74–78 Marcellus asks if anyone can tell him why the Danish people (***subject of the land***) must weary themselves each night (***nightly toils***) with sentry duty and why there is so much casting of armaments (***brazen cannon***) and foreign trade (***mart***) for weapons.

81 ***toward:*** approaching, in preparation.

83–104 Stirred by jealousy (***emulate pride***), Fortinbras challenged Hamlet to combat and was killed. By prior agreement (***sealed compact***) and according to the laws governing combat (***heraldry***), Hamlet gained all the land that Fortinbras had possessed (***stood seized of***). Hamlet had pledged (***gagèd***) an equivalent portion (***moiety competent***) of his land, which would have

(continued on page 14)

What think you on 't?

60 **Horatio.** Before my God, I might not this believe
Without the sensible and true avouch
Of mine own eyes.

Marcellus.   Is it not like the King?

Horatio. As thou art to thyself.
Such was the very armor he had on
65 When he the ambitious Norway combated.
So frowned he once when, in an angry parle,
He smote the sledded Polacks on the ice.
'Tis strange.

Marcellus. Thus twice before, and jump at this dead hour,
70 With martial stalk hath he gone by our watch.

Horatio. In what particular thought to work I know not,
But in the gross and scope of mine opinion
This bodes some strange eruption to our state.

Marcellus. Good now, sit down, and tell me, he that
knows,
75 Why this same strict and most observant watch
So nightly toils the subject of the land,
And why such daily cast of brazen cannon
And foreign mart for implements of war,
Why such impress of shipwrights, whose sore task
80 Does not divide the Sunday from the week.
What might be toward that this sweaty haste
Doth make the night joint laborer with the day?
Who is 't that can inform me?

Horatio.   That can I.
At least the whisper goes so: our last king,
85 Whose image even but now appeared to us,
Was, as you know, by Fortinbras of Norway,
Thereto pricked on by a most emulate pride,
Dared to the combat; in which our valiant Hamlet
(For so this side of our known world esteemed him)
90 Did slay this Fortinbras, who by a sealed compact,

gone to Fortinbras if he won the battle, as was speci-fied in the same agreement (*comart and carriage of the article designed*) that gave Fortinbras's land to Hamlet. Young Fortinbras (the late king's son), who has an undisciplined character (*unimprovèd mettle*), has gathered hastily (*Sharked up*) in outlying districts (*skirts*) of Norway a troop of lawless desperadoes to serve in some undertaking that requires courage (*hath a stomach in 't*).

110 *head:* source.

111 *rummage:* bustle.

113 *Well . . . sort:* it may be fitting.

116 *mote:* speck of dust.

117 *palmy:* thriving, flourishing.

119 *sheeted:* wrapped in shrouds.

120 *gibber:* chatter. (The confusing transition between this line and the next suggests that one or more lines are missing.)

122 *disasters:* menacing signs; *moist star:* the moon, which controls the Earth's tides.

123 *Neptune:* Roman god of the sea.

125–129 A similar foreshadowing (*precurse*) has occurred in Denmark, where a terrible event (*omen*) was preceded by signs that were like forerunners (*harbingers*) announcing the approach of someone.

Well ratified by law and heraldry,
Did forfeit, with his life, all those his lands
Which he stood seized of, to the conqueror.
Against the which a moiety competent
95 Was gagèd by our king, which had returned
To the inheritance of Fortinbras
Had he been vanquisher, as, by the same comart
And carriage of the article designed,
His fell to Hamlet. Now, sir, young Fortinbras,
100 Of unimprovèd mettle hot and full,
Hath in the skirts of Norway here and there
Sharked up a list of lawless resolutes
For food and diet to some enterprise
That hath a stomach in 't; which is no other
105 (As it doth well appear unto our state)
But to recover of us, by strong hand
And terms compulsatory, those foresaid lands
So by his father lost. And this, I take it,
Is the main motive of our preparations,
110 The source of this our watch, and the chief head
Of this posthaste and rummage in the land.

Barnardo. I think it be no other but e'en so.
Well may it sort that this portentous figure
Comes armèd through our watch so like the king
115 That was and is the question of these wars.

Horatio. A mote it is to trouble the mind's eye.
In the most high and palmy state of Rome,
A little ere the mightiest Julius fell,
The graves stood tenantless, and the sheeted dead
120 Did squeak and gibber in the Roman streets;
As stars with trains of fire and dews of blood,
Disasters in the sun; and the moist star,
Upon whose influence Neptune's empire stands,
Was sick almost to doomsday with eclipse.
125 And even the like precurse of feared events,
As harbingers preceding still the fates
And prologue to the omen coming on,

130 *soft:* be quiet, hold off.

131 *cross:* confront.

138 *happily . . . avoid:* perhaps (*happily*) may be avoided if known in advance.

141 *extorted:* ill-gotten.

144 *partisan:* a long-handled weapon.

154 *started:* made a sudden movement.

Have heaven and earth together demonstrated
Unto our climatures and countrymen.

[*Enter* Ghost.]

130   But soft, behold! Lo, where it comes again!
I'll cross it though it blast me.—Stay, illusion!

[*It spreads his arms.*]

If thou hast any sound or use of voice,
Speak to me.
If there be any good thing to be done
135   That may to thee do ease and grace to me,
Speak to me.
If thou art privy to thy country's fate,
Which happily foreknowing may avoid,
O, speak!
140   Or if thou hast uphoarded in thy life
Extorted treasure in the womb of earth,
For which, they say, you spirits oft walk in death,
Speak of it.
[*The cock crows.*]
                    Stay and speak!—Stop it, Marcellus.

Marcellus. Shall I strike it with my partisan?

145   **Horatio.** Do, if it will not stand.

Barnardo. 'Tis here.

Horatio. 'Tis here.

[Ghost *exits.*]

Marcellus. 'Tis gone.
We do it wrong, being so majestical,
150   To offer it the show of violence,
For it is as the air, invulnerable,
And our vain blows malicious mockery.

Barnardo. It was about to speak when the cock crew.

Horatio. And then it started like a guilty thing

160 *extravagant and erring:* wandering out of bounds.

162 *made probation:* demonstrated.

164–165 *ever . . . celebrated:* just before Christmas.

168 *strike:* put forth an evil influence.
169 *takes:* bewitches.

155 Upon a fearful summons. I have heard
The cock, that is the trumpet to the morn,
Doth with his lofty and shrill-sounding throat
Awake the god of day, and at his warning,
Whether in sea or fire, in earth or air,
160 Th' extravagant and erring spirit hies
To his confine, and of the truth herein
This present object made probation.

Marcellus. It faded on the crowing of the cock.
Some say that ever 'gainst that season comes
165 Wherein our Savior's birth is celebrated,
This bird of dawning singeth all night long;
And then, they say, no spirit dare stir abroad,
The nights are wholesome; then no planets strike,
No fairy takes, nor witch hath power to charm,
170 So hallowed and so gracious is that time.

Horatio. So have I heard and do in part believe it.
But look, the morn in russet mantle clad
Walks o'er the dew of yon high eastward hill.
Break we our watch up, and by my advice
175 Let us impart what we have seen tonight
Unto young Hamlet; for, upon my life,
This spirit, dumb to us, will speak to him.
Do you consent we shall acquaint him with it
As needful in our loves, fitting our duty?

180 **Marcellus.** Let's do 't, I pray, and I this morning know
Where we shall find him most convenient.

[*They exit.*]

8 ***our sometime sister:*** my former sister-in-law. (Claudius uses the royal "we.")

9 ***jointress:*** a woman who owns property with her husband.

11–12 ***With . . . eye:*** with one eye reflecting good fortune and the other eye, sorrow; ***dirge:*** a song of mourning. *Notice how Claudius balances one element against another in this speech. What impression do you think he's trying to make?*

17–20 Claudius says that Fortinbras either holds him in low regard or thinks that Denmark is in disarray after the death of King Hamlet.

Scene 2 *A state room at the castle.*

*Claudius, the new King of Denmark, makes a formal
appearance at court. He thanks his supporters and
announces that he is sending ambassadors to Norway to
head off a threatened attack by Fortinbras. Claudius gives
Laertes, the son of his advisor Polonius, permission to
return to France. He then chides Hamlet for his excessive
mourning. Hamlet reluctantly agrees to stay at Elsinore
instead of returning to study at Wittenberg. Alone, he
expresses his disgust over his mother's hasty marriage to
Claudius, her late husband's brother. Horatio, Bernardo,
and Marcellus arrive and tell him about the Ghost.
Hamlet decides to join them on their watch that night.*

[*Flourish. Enter* Claudius, *King of Denmark,* Gertrude the
Queen, *the* Council, *as* Polonius, *and his son* Laertes,
Hamlet, *with others, among them* Voltemand *and*
Cornelius.]

King. Though yet of Hamlet our dear brother's death
　　The memory be green, and that it us befitted
　　To bear our hearts in grief, and our whole kingdom
　　To be contracted in one brow of woe,
5　　Yet so far hath discretion fought with nature
　　That we with wisest sorrow think on him
　　Together with remembrance of ourselves.
　　Therefore our sometime sister, now our queen,
　　Th' imperial jointress to this warlike state,
10　　Have we (as 'twere with a defeated joy,
　　With an auspicious and a dropping eye,
　　With mirth in funeral and with dirge in marriage,
　　In equal scale weighing delight and dole)
　　Taken to wife. Nor have we herein barred
15　　Your better wisdoms, which have freely gone
　　With this affair along. For all, our thanks.
　　Now follows that you know. Young Fortinbras,
　　Holding a weak supposal of our worth
　　Or thinking by our late dear brother's death

21 *Colleaguèd . . . advantage:* connected with this false hope of his superior position.

23 *Importing:* relating to.

29 *impotent:* helpless.

30–33 Since Fortinbras has obtained all of his troops and supplies from Norway, Claudius has asked the King of Norway to stop him from proceeding further.

37 *To business:* to negotiate.

38 *dilated articles:* detailed instructions.

45 *lose your voice:* waste your breath.

47 *native:* closely connected.

20 Our state to be disjoint and out of frame,
Colleaguèd with this dream of his advantage,
He hath not failed to pester us with message
Importing the surrender of those lands
Lost by his father, with all bonds of law,
25 To our most valiant brother—so much for him.
Now for ourself and for this time of meeting.
Thus much the business is: we have here writ
To Norway, uncle of young Fortinbras,
Who, impotent and bedrid, scarcely hears
30 Of this his nephew's purpose, to suppress
His further gait herein, in that the levies,
The lists, and full proportions are all made
Out of his subject; and we here dispatch
You, good Cornelius, and you, Voltemand,
35 For bearers of this greeting to old Norway,
Giving to you no further personal power
To business with the King more than the scope
Of these dilated articles allow.

[*Giving them a paper.*]

Farewell, and let your haste commend your duty.

40 **Cornelius/Voltemand.** In that and all things will we
show our duty.

King. We doubt it nothing. Heartily farewell.

[*Voltemand and* Cornelius *exit.*]

And now, Laertes, what's the news with you?
You told us of some suit. What is 't, Laertes?
You cannot speak of reason to the Dane
45 And lose your voice. What wouldst thou beg, Laertes,
That shall not be my offer, not thy asking?
The head is not more native to the heart,
The hand more instrumental to the mouth,
Than is the throne of Denmark to thy father.
50 What wouldst thou have, Laertes?

Laertes. My dread lord,

60 *Upon . . . consent:* I reluctantly agreed to his wishes.

62–63 Claudius gives him permission to leave and hopes that his finest qualities (*best graces*) guide his behavior.

64 *cousin:* kinsman.

65 Hamlet plays off two meanings of *kind:* "loving" and "natural." Although he is Claudius's stepson as well as his nephew (*more than kin*), Hamlet does not resemble him in nature or feel a son's affection for him.

67 *sun:* the sunlight of royal favor (also a pun on *son,* suggesting annoyance at Claudius's use of the word).

68 *nighted color:* black mourning clothes, dark mood.

70 *vailèd lids:* lowered eyes.

74 Hamlet plays off two meanings of *common:* "universal" and "vulgar."

75 *particular:* special, personal.

77–83 Hamlet's feelings are not limited to the black mourning clothes he wears, his heavy sighs (*windy suspiration of forced breath*), his tears (*fruitful river in the eye*), the downcast expression on his face (*dejected havior of the visage*), and other outward expressions of grief.

Your leave and favor to return to France,
From whence though willingly I came to Denmark
To show my duty in your coronation,
Yet now I must confess, that duty done,
55 My thoughts and wishes bend again toward France
And bow them to your gracious leave and pardon.

King. Have you your father's leave? What says Polonius?

Polonius. Hath, my lord, wrung from me my slow leave
By laborsome petition, and at last
60 Upon his will I sealed my hard consent.
I do beseech you give him leave to go.

King. Take thy fair hour, Laertes. Time be thine,
And thy best graces spend it at thy will.—
But now, my cousin Hamlet and my son—

65 **Hamlet** [*aside*]. A little more than kin and less than kind.

King. How is it that the clouds still hang on you?

Hamlet. Not so, my lord; I am too much in the sun.

Queen. Good Hamlet, cast thy nighted color off,
And let thine eye look like a friend on Denmark.
70 Do not forever with thy vailèd lids
Seek for thy noble father in the dust.
Thou know'st 'tis common; all that lives must die,
Passing through nature to eternity.

Hamlet. Ay, madam, it is common.

Queen.   If it be,
75 Why seems it so particular with thee?

Hamlet. "Seems," madam? Nay, it is. I know not "seems."
'Tis not alone my inky cloak, good mother,
Nor customary suits of solemn black,
Nor windy suspiration of forced breath,
80 No, nor the fruitful river in the eye,
Nor the dejected havior of the visage,
Together with all forms, moods, shapes of grief,

89–94 Claudius says that a surviving son must dutifully mourn (*do obsequious sorrow*) for a while, but to remain stubbornly in grief (*obstinate condolement*) beyond that appropriate period is perverse.

96 *unfortified:* unstrengthened against adversity.

99 *As . . . sense:* as the most common experience.

104 *still:* always.

105 *corse:* corpse.

107 *unprevailing:* not yielding to persuasion.

108–112 Claudius claims that he offers (*impart toward*) Hamlet, who is next in line (*most immediate*) to succeed to the throne, all the love that the most affectionate father feels for his son. *Does he seem sincere?*

113 Wittenberg University (founded in 1502) was famous for being the school of German theologian Martin Luther, whose challenge to Roman Catholic doctrine started the Reformation.

114 *retrograde:* contrary.

That can denote me truly. These indeed "seem,"
For they are actions that a man might play;
85 But I have that within which passes show,
These but the trappings and the suits of woe.

King. 'Tis sweet and commendable in your nature,
   Hamlet,
To give these mourning duties to your father.
But you must know your father lost a father,
90 That father lost, lost his, and the survivor bound
In filial obligation for some term
To do obsequious sorrow. But to persever
In obstinate condolement is a course
Of impious stubbornness. 'Tis unmanly grief.
95 It shows a will most incorrect to heaven,
A heart unfortified, a mind impatient,
An understanding simple and unschooled.
For what we know must be and is as common
As any the most vulgar thing to sense,
100 Why should we in our peevish opposition
Take it to heart? Fie, 'tis a fault to heaven,
A fault against the dead, a fault to nature,
To reason most absurd, whose common theme
Is death of fathers, and who still hath cried,
105 From the first corse till he that died today,
"This must be so." We pray you, throw to earth
This unprevailing woe and think of us
As of a father; for let the world take note,
You are the most immediate to our throne,
110 And with no less nobility of love
Than that which dearest father bears his son
Do I impart toward you. For your intent
In going back to school in Wittenberg,
It is most retrograde to our desire,
115 And we beseech you, bend you to remain
Here in the cheer and comfort of our eye,
Our chiefest courtier, cousin, and our son.

Queen. Let not thy mother lose her prayers, Hamlet.

125-128 Claudius boasts that he (***Denmark***) will not merely drink a happy toast (***jocund health***) that day, but a deep drink (***rouse***) accompanied by fanfare, which heaven will echo with thunder.

129 *sullied:* stained, defiled.

132 *canon:* law.

137 *merely:* entirely.

139–140 Hamlet says that comparing his father to Claudius would be like comparing the sun god ***Hyperion*** to a ***satyr*** (a mythical creature, half man and half goat, associated with lechery).

141 *beteem:* allow.

147 *or ere:* before.

149 *Niobe:* a Greek mythological figure who continued weeping for her slaughtered children even after she was turned to stone.

150 *wants . . . reason:* does not possess the ability to reason.

I pray thee, stay with us. Go not to Wittenberg.

120 **Hamlet.** I shall in all my best obey you, madam.

King. Why, 'tis a loving and a fair reply.
   Be as ourself in Denmark.—Madam, come.
   This gentle and unforced accord of Hamlet
   Sits smiling to my heart, in grace whereof
125 No jocund health that Denmark drinks today
   But the great cannon to the clouds shall tell,
   And the King's rouse the heaven shall bruit again,
   Respeaking earthly thunder. Come away.

[*Flourish. All but* Hamlet *exit.*]

Hamlet. O, that this too, too sullied flesh would melt,
130 Thaw, and resolve itself into a dew,
   Or that the Everlasting had not fixed
   His canon 'gainst self-slaughter! O God, God,
   How weary, stale, flat, and unprofitable
   Seem to me all the uses of this world!
135 Fie on 't, ah fie! 'Tis an unweeded garden
   That grows to seed. Things rank and gross in nature
   Possess it merely. That it should come to this:
   But two months dead—nay, not so much, not two.
   So excellent a king, that was to this
140 Hyperion to a satyr; so loving to my mother
   That he might not beteem the winds of heaven
   Visit her face too roughly. Heaven and earth,
   Must I remember? Why, she would hang on him
   As if increase of appetite had grown
145 By what it fed on. And yet, within a month
   (Let me not think on 't; frailty, thy name is woman!),
   A little month, or ere those shoes were old
   With which she followed my poor father's body,
   Like Niobe, all tears—why she, even she
150 (O God, a beast that wants discourse of reason
   Would have mourned longer!), married with my
      uncle,
   My father's brother, but no more like my father

153 *Hercules:* in Greek mythology, a hero of great strength; ***Within a month:*** Notice how Hamlet continues to shorten the period of mourning (see lines 138 and 145).

155 *Had . . . eyes:* had stopped reddening her inflamed (*gallèd*) eyes.

157 *incestuous:* Marriage between a widow and her late husband's brother was often considered incestuous in Shakespeare's time and was prohibited by church law.

163–164 Horatio refers to himself as a "servant" out of respect for Hamlet's position, but Hamlet insists that they call each other "friend."

169 *what . . . from:* what are you doing away from.

173 *truster:* believer.

180 *hard upon:* soon after.

181–182 *The funeral . . . tables:* Leftovers from the funeral were served cold at the marriage feast.

Than I to Hercules. Within a month,
Ere yet the salt of most unrighteous tears
155 Had left the flushing in her gallèd eyes,
She married. O, most wicked speed, to post
With such dexterity to incestuous sheets!
It is not, nor it cannot come to good.
But break, my heart, for I must hold my tongue.

[*Enter* Horatio, Marcellus, *and* Barnardo.]

160 **Horatio.** Hail to your lordship.

Hamlet. I am glad to see you well.
Horatio—or I do forget myself!

Horatio. The same, my lord, and your poor servant ever.

Hamlet. Sir, my good friend. I'll change that name
with you.
165 And what make you from Wittenberg, Horatio?—
Marcellus?

Marcellus. My good lord.

Hamlet. I am very glad to see you. [*To* Barnardo.] Good
even, sir.—
But what, in faith, make you from Wittenberg?

170 **Horatio.** A truant disposition, good my lord.

Hamlet. I would not hear your enemy say so,
Nor shall you do my ear that violence
To make it truster of your own report
Against yourself. I know you are no truant.
175 But what is your affair in Elsinore?
We'll teach you to drink deep ere you depart.

Horatio. My lord, I came to see your father's funeral.

Hamlet. I prithee, do not mock me, fellow student.
I think it was to see my mother's wedding.

180 **Horatio.** Indeed, my lord, it followed hard upon.

Hamlet. Thrift, thrift, Horatio. The funeral baked meats

183 *dearest:* most hated.

184 *Or ever:* before.

187 *goodly:* fine, admirable.

193–194 *Season . . . ear:* Control your astonishment for a moment and listen carefully.

201 *Armèd . . . cap-à-pie:* armed properly in every detail, from head to foot.

205 *Within his truncheon's length:* no farther away than the length of his short staff.

205–206 *distilled . . . fear:* reduced almost to jelly by fear.

207–208 *This . . . did:* They told me this in terrified (*dreadful*) secrecy.

210 *delivered:* asserted.

Did coldly furnish forth the marriage tables.
Would I had met my dearest foe in heaven
Or ever I had seen that day, Horatio!
185 My father—methinks I see my father.

Horatio. Where, my lord?

Hamlet.   In my mind's eye, Horatio.

Horatio. I saw him once. He was a goodly king.

Hamlet. He was a man. Take him for all in all,
I shall not look upon his like again.

190 **Horatio.** My lord, I think I saw him yesternight.

Hamlet. Saw who?

Horatio. My lord, the King your father.

Hamlet.   The King my father?

Horatio. Season your admiration for a while
With an attent ear, till I may deliver
195 Upon the witness of these gentlemen
This marvel to you.

Hamlet.   For God's love, let me hear!

Horatio Two nights together had these gentlemen,
Marcellus and Barnardo, on their watch,
In the dead waste and middle of the night,
200 Been thus encountered: a figure like your father,
Armèd at point exactly, cap-à-pie,
Appears before them and with solemn march
Goes slow and stately by them. Thrice he walked
By their oppressed and fear-surprisèd eyes
205 Within his truncheon's length, whilst they, distilled
Almost to jelly with the act of fear,
Stand dumb and speak not to him. This to me
In dreadful secrecy impart they did,
And I with them the third night kept the watch,
210 Where, as they had delivered, both in time,
Form of the thing (each word made true and good),

217–218 *did . . . speak:* began to move as if it were going to speak.

219 *even then:* just then.

230 *beaver:* movable front piece of a helmet.

The apparition comes. I knew your father;
These hands are not more like.

Hamlet.   But where was this?

Marcellus. My lord, upon the platform where we watch.

215 **Hamlet.** Did you not speak to it?

Horatio.   My lord, I did,
But answer made it none. Yet once methought
It lifted up its head and did address
Itself to motion, like as it would speak;
But even then the morning cock crew loud,
220 And at the sound it shrunk in haste away
And vanished from our sight.

Hamlet.   'Tis very strange.

Horatio. As I do live, my honored lord, 'tis true.
And we did think it writ down in our duty
To let you know of it.

225 **Hamlet.** Indeed, sirs, but this troubles me.
Hold you the watch tonight?

All.   We do, my lord.

Hamlet. Armed, say you?

All.   Armed, my lord.

Hamlet.   From top to toe?
All My lord, from head to foot.

Hamlet. Then saw you not his face?

230 **Horatio.** O, yes, my lord, he wore his beaver up.

Hamlet. What, looked he frowningly?

Horatio. A countenance more in sorrow than in anger.

Hamlet. Pale or red?

Horatio. Nay, very pale.

238–239 *While . . . hundred:* for as long as one could count (*tell*) to one hundred at a moderate pace.

240 *grizzled:* gray.

242 *A sable silvered:* black hair with white hair mixed through it.

248 *tenable:* held.

249 *whatsomever:* whatever; *hap:* happen.

251 *I . . . loves:* I will reward your devotion.

256 *doubt:* suspect.

Hamlet. And fixed his eyes upon you?

235 **Horatio.** Most constantly.

Hamlet. I would I had been there.

Horatio. It would have much amazed you.

Hamlet. Very like. Stayed it long?

Horatio. While one with moderate haste might tell a
hundred.

Barnardo/Marcellus. Longer, longer.

240 **Horatio.** Not when I saw 't.

Hamlet. His beard was grizzled, no?

Horatio. It was as I have seen it in his life,
A sable silvered.

Hamlet. I will watch tonight.
Perchance 'twill walk again.

Horatio. I warrant it will.

Hamlet. If it assume my noble father's person,
245 I'll speak to it, though hell itself should gape
And bid me hold my peace. I pray you all,
If you have hitherto concealed this sight,
Let it be tenable in your silence still;
And whatsomever else shall hap tonight,
250 Give it an understanding but no tongue.
I will requite your loves. So fare you well.
Upon the platform, 'twixt eleven and twelve,
I'll visit you.

All. Our duty to your Honor.

Hamlet. Your loves, as mine to you. Farewell.

[*All but* Hamlet *exit.*]

255 My father's spirit—in arms! All is not well.
I doubt some foul play. Would the night were come!

1–4 Laertes tells Ophelia to write to him as long as ships are available to carry her letters.

6 *fashion . . . blood:* a temporary enthusiasm and an amorous whim.

7 *in . . . nature:* at the beginning of its prime.

8 *Forward:* early blooming.

9–10 *The . . . more*: a sweet but temporary diversion.

11–14 A growing person does not only increase in strength (*thews*) and size, but as the body grows (*this temple waxes*), the inner life (*inward service*) of mind and soul grows along with it.

15 *cautel:* deceit.

17 *His . . . weighed:* if you consider his high position.

Till then, sit still, my soul. Foul deeds will rise,
Though all the earth o'erwhelm them, to men's eyes.

[*He exits.*]

Scene 3 *Polonius's chambers.*

*While saying goodbye to his sister, Ophelia, Laertes warns
her not to trust Hamlet's declarations of love. Polonius
enters the room and gives Laertes tedious advice on how
to behave in France. After Laertes leaves, Polonius
questions his daughter. Agreeing with Laertes, he forbids
her to speak to Hamlet.*

[*Enter* Laertes *and* Ophelia, *his sister.*]

Laertes. My necessaries are embarked. Farewell.
  And, sister, as the winds give benefit
  And convey is assistant, do not sleep,
  But let me hear from you.

Ophelia.   Do you doubt that?

5 **Laertes.** For Hamlet, and the trifling of his favor,
  Hold it a fashion and a toy in blood,
  A violet in the youth of primy nature,
  Forward, not permanent, sweet, not lasting,
  The perfume and suppliance of a minute,
10   No more.

Ophelia.   No more but so?

Laertes.   Think it no more.
  For nature, crescent, does not grow alone
  In thews and bulk, but, as this temple waxes,
  The inward service of the mind and soul
  Grows wide withal. Perhaps he loves you now,
15   And now no soil nor cautel doth besmirch
  The virtue of his will; but you must fear,
  His greatness weighed, his will is not his own,

20 Carve: choose.

22–24 And . . . head: His choice must be limited (**circum-scribed**) by the opinion and consent (**voice and yield-ing**) of Denmark.

24–28 Laertes tells her to believe Hamlet's love declarations only to the extent that someone in Hamlet's position can act on his words, which is limited by the need for Denmark's approval.

30 credent: trustful; **list:** listen to.

31–32 your chaste . . . importunity: lose your virginity to his uncontrolled pleading.

34 keep . . . affection: Don't go as far as your emotions would lead you.

36 chariest: most careful; **prodigal:** reckless.

39 canker galls: cankerworm destroys; **infants:** early flowers.

40 buttons: buds; **disclosed:** opened.

42 contagious blastments: withering blights, harm or injury, catastrophes.

44 Youth . . . near: Youth by nature is prone to rebel.

46–51 Ophelia warns him not to act like a hypocritical pastor, preaching virtue and abstinence while leading a life of promiscuity and ignoring his own advice.

For he himself is subject to his birth.
He may not, as unvalued persons do,
20 Carve for himself, for on his choice depends
The safety and the health of this whole state.
And therefore must his choice be circumscribed
Unto the voice and yielding of that body
Whereof he is the head. Then, if he says he loves you,
25 It fits your wisdom so far to believe it
As he in his particular act and place
May give his saying deed, which is no further
Than the main voice of Denmark goes withal.
Then weigh what loss your honor may sustain
30 If with too credent ear you list his songs
Or lose your heart or your chaste treasure open
To his unmastered importunity.
Fear it, Ophelia; fear it, my dear sister,
And keep you in the rear of your affection,
35 Out of the shot and danger of desire.
The chariest maid is prodigal enough
If she unmask her beauty to the moon.
Virtue itself 'scapes not calumnious strokes.
The canker galls the infants of the spring
40 Too oft before their buttons be disclosed,
And, in the morn and liquid dew of youth,
Contagious blastments are most imminent.
Be wary, then; best safety lies in fear.
Youth to itself rebels, though none else near.

45 **Ophelia.** I shall the effect of this good lesson keep
As watchman to my heart. But, good my brother,
Do not, as some ungracious pastors do,
Show me the steep and thorny way to heaven,
Whiles, like a puffed and reckless libertine,
50 Himself the primrose path of dalliance treads
And recks not his own rede.

Laertes. O, fear me not.

[*Enter* Polonius.]

58–65 Polonius tells Laertes to write down (***character***) these few rules of conduct (***precepts***) in his memory. He should keep his thoughts to himself and not act on any unfit (***unproportioned***) thoughts, be friendly but not vulgar, remain loyal to friends proven (***tried***) worthy of being accepted but not shake hands with every swaggering youth (***unfledged courage***) who comes along.

73–74 ***And they . . . that:*** Upper-class French people especially show their refinement and nobility in their choice of apparel.

77 ***husbandry:*** thrift, proper handling of money.

81 Polonius hopes that his advice will ripen (***season***) in Laertes.

55–81 *What do you think is going through Laertes's mind during this long speech by his father?*

83 ***invests:*** is pressing.

I stay too long. But here my father comes.
A double blessing is a double grace.
Occasion smiles upon a second leave.

55 **Polonius.** Yet here, Laertes? Aboard, aboard, for shame!
The wind sits in the shoulder of your sail,
And you are stayed for. There, my blessing with thee.
And these few precepts in thy memory
Look thou character. Give thy thoughts no tongue,
60 Nor any unproportioned thought his act.
Be thou familiar, but by no means vulgar.
Those friends thou hast, and their adoption tried,
Grapple them unto thy soul with hoops of steel,
But do not dull thy palm with entertainment
65 Of each new-hatched, unfledged courage. Beware
Of entrance to a quarrel, but, being in,
Bear 't that th' opposèd may beware of thee.
Give every man thy ear, but few thy voice.
Take each man's censure, but reserve thy judgment.
70 Costly thy habit as thy purse can buy,
But not expressed in fancy (rich, not gaudy),
For the apparel oft proclaims the man,
And they in France of the best rank and station
Are of a most select and generous chief in that.
75 Neither a borrower nor a lender be,
For loan oft loses both itself and friend,
And borrowing dulls the edge of husbandry.
This above all: to thine own self be true,
And it must follow, as the night the day,
80 Thou canst not then be false to any man.
Farewell. My blessing season this in thee.

Laertes. Most humbly do I take my leave, my lord.

Polonius. The time invests you. Go, your servants tend.

Laertes. Farewell, Ophelia, and remember well
85 What I have said to you.

Ophelia. 'Tis in my memory locked,
And you yourself shall keep the key of it.

91 *Marry:* a mild oath, shortened from
"by the Virgin Mary."

95 *put on:* told to.

100–110 *Tenders:* offers (lines 100 and 104). Polonius uses the
word in line 107 to refer to coins that are not legal cur-
rency (*sterling*). He then warns Ophelia to offer (*tender*) herself at a higher rate (*more dearly*), or she will
tender Polonius a fool—meaning either that she will
present herself as a fool, that she will make him look
like a fool, or that she will give him a grandchild.

116 *springes . . . woodcocks:* snares to catch birds that
are easily caught.

Laertes. Farewell.

[Laertes *exits.*]

Polonius. What is 't, Ophelia, he hath said to you?

90 **Ophelia.** So please you, something touching the Lord
    Hamlet.

Polonius. Marry, well bethought.
    'Tis told me he hath very oft of late
    Given private time to you, and you yourself
    Have of your audience been most free and bounteous.
95   If it be so (as so 'tis put on me,
    And that in way of caution), I must tell you
    You do not understand yourself so clearly
    As it behooves my daughter and your honor.
    What is between you? Give me up the truth.

100 **Ophelia.** He hath, my lord, of late made many tenders
    Of his affection to me.

Polonius. Affection, puh! You speak like a green girl
    Unsifted in such perilous circumstance.
    Do you believe his "tenders," as you call them?

105 **Ophelia.** I do not know, my lord, what I should think.

Polonius. Marry, I will teach you. Think yourself a baby
    That you have ta'en these tenders for true pay,
    Which are not sterling. Tender yourself more dearly,
    Or (not to crack the wind of the poor phrase,
110   Running it thus) you'll tender me a fool.

Ophelia. My lord, he hath importuned me with love
    In honorable fashion—

Polonius. Ay, "fashion" you may call it. Go to, go to!

Ophelia. And hath given countenance to his speech,
    my lord,
115   With almost all the holy vows of heaven.

Polonius. Ay, springes to catch woodcocks. I do know,

117 *prodigal:* lavishly.

118–121 *These blazes . . . fire:* These blazes, which lose their light and heat almost immediately, should not be mistaken for fire.

123–135 Polonius, metaphorically referring to Ophelia as a besieged castle, tells her not to enter into negotiations (*entreatments*) for surrender merely because the enemy wants to meet (*parle*) with her. Hamlet's vows are go-betweens (*brokers*) that are not like their outward appearance; these solicitors (*implorators*) of sinful petitions (*unholy suits*) speak in pious terms in order to deceive. Polonius orders her never to disgrace (*slander*) a moment of her time by speaking to Hamlet. *How would you describe Polonius's manner of speaking?*

1 *shrewdly:* keenly.

2 *eager:* cutting.

When the blood burns, how prodigal the soul
Lends the tongue vows. These blazes, daughter,
Giving more light than heat, extinct in both
120 Even in their promise as it is a-making,
You must not take for fire. From this time
Be something scanter of your maiden presence.
Set your entreatments at a higher rate
Than a command to parle. For Lord Hamlet,
125 Believe so much in him that he is young,
And with a larger tether may he walk
Than may be given you. In few, Ophelia,
Do not believe his vows, for they are brokers,
Not of that dye which their investments show,
130 But mere implorators of unholy suits,
Breathing like sanctified and pious bawds
The better to beguile. This is for all:
I would not, in plain terms, from this time forth
Have you so slander any moment leisure
135 As to give words or talk with the Lord Hamlet.
Look to 't, I charge you. Come your ways.

Ophelia. I shall obey, my lord.

[*They exit.*]

Scene 4 *A guard platform at the castle.*

*The Ghost appears before Hamlet, Horatio, and
Marcellus. Hamlet tries to find out the reason for this
visit. When the Ghost beckons, Hamlet insists on
following it, despite his friends' objections.*

[*Enter* Hamlet, Horatio, *and* Marcellus.]

Hamlet. The air bites shrewdly; it is very cold.

Horatio. It is a nipping and an eager air.

Hamlet. What hour now?

9–13 The King stays up tonight drinking (***keeps wassail***) and dancing wildly (***the swagg'ring upspring reels***); as he drinks down a glass of Rhine wine all at once, this feat is celebrated by the playing of kettledrums and trumpets.

17 ***to the manner born:*** familiar since birth with this custom.

19–24 This drunken (***heavy-headed***) festivity everywhere makes us slandered and blamed by other nations. They call us drunkards and pigs, soiling our good name. Even when we do something outstanding, the essence of our reputation (***pith and marrow of our attribute***) is lost through drunkenness.

26 ***mole:*** defect.

29–32 Hamlet metaphorically describes reason as a castle whose fortified walls (***pales and forts***) are broken by the excessive growth of a natural trait or characteristic (***complexion***) or by a habit that corrupts one's manners.

34 ***nature's livery:*** a defect they are born with (literally, a uniform provided by nature); ***fortune's star:*** the effect of fortune or destiny, a defect they acquire.

35 ***His virtues else:*** their other virtues.

Horatio. I think it lacks of twelve.

5 **Marcellus.** No, it is struck.

Horatio. Indeed, I heard it not. It then draws near the
season
Wherein the spirit held his wont to walk.

[*A flourish of trumpets and two pieces goes off.*]

What does this mean, my lord?

Hamlet. The King doth wake tonight and takes his
rouse,
10 Keeps wassail, and the swagg'ring upspring reels;
And, as he drains his draughts of Rhenish down,
The kettledrum and trumpet thus bray out
The triumph of his pledge.

Horatio. Is it a custom?

15 **Hamlet.** Ay, marry, is 't,
But, to my mind, though I am native here
And to the manner born, it is a custom
More honored in the breach than the observance.
This heavy-headed revel east and west
20 Makes us traduced and taxed of other nations.
They clepe us drunkards and with swinish phrase
Soil our addition. And, indeed, it takes
From our achievements, though performed at height,
The pith and marrow of our attribute.
25 So oft it chances in particular men
That for some vicious mole of nature in them,
As in their birth (wherein they are not guilty,
Since nature cannot choose his origin),
By the o'ergrowth of some complexion
30 (Oft breaking down the pales and forts of reason),
Or by some habit that too much o'erleavens
The form of plausive manners—that these men,
Carrying, I say, the stamp of one defect,
Being nature's livery or fortune's star,
35 His virtues else, be they as pure as grace,

38–40 ***The dram . . . scandal:*** A small amount of evil blots out all of a person's good qualities.

45 ***questionable:*** capable of responding to questions.

48–50 ***tell . . . cerements:*** Tell me why your bones, which were placed in a coffin and received a proper church burial, have escaped from their burial clothes.

57 ***horridly . . . disposition:*** disturb us terribly.

61–62 ***As if . . . alone:*** as if it has something to tell you on your own.

As infinite as man may undergo,
Shall in the general censure take corruption
From that particular fault. The dram of evil
Doth all the noble substance of a doubt
40 To his own scandal.

[*Enter* Ghost.]

Horatio.   Look, my lord, it comes.

Hamlet. Angels and ministers of grace, defend us!
Be thou a spirit of health or goblin damned,
Bring with thee airs from heaven or blasts from hell,
Be thy intents wicked or charitable,
45 Thou com'st in such a questionable shape
That I will speak to thee. I'll call thee "Hamlet,"
"King," "Father," "Royal Dane." O, answer me!
Let me not burst in ignorance, but tell
Why thy canonized bones, hearsèd in death,
50 Have burst their cerements; why the sepulcher,
Wherein we saw thee quietly interred,
Hath oped his ponderous and marble jaws
To cast thee up again. What may this mean
That thou, dead corse, again in complete steel,
55 Revisits thus the glimpses of the moon,
Making night hideous, and we fools of nature
So horridly to shake our disposition
With thoughts beyond the reaches of our souls?
Say, why is this? Wherefore? What should we do?

[Ghost *beckons*.]

60 **Horatio.** It beckons you to go away with it
As if it some impartment did desire
To you alone.

Marcellus.   Look with what courteous action
It waves you to a more removèd ground.
But do not go with it.

Horatio.   No, by no means.

67 *pin's fee:* the value of a pin.

71–76 Horatio is worried that the Ghost might lead Hamlet toward the sea (***flood***) or to the top of the cliff that hangs (***beetles***) over the sea, and then take on some horrible appearance that would drive Hamlet insane. *What does he fear the Ghost might actually be?*

77 *toys of desperation:* irrational impulses.

84 *arture:* artery.

85 *Nemean lion's nerve:* the sinews of a mythical lion strangled by Hercules.

87 *lets:* hinders.

91 *Have after:* Let's go after him.

65 **Hamlet.** It will not speak. Then I will follow it.

Horatio. Do not, my lord.

Hamlet.   Why, what should be the fear?
I do not set my life at a pin's fee.
And for my soul, what can it do to that,
Being a thing immortal as itself?
70 It waves me forth again. I'll follow it.

Horatio. What if it tempt you toward the flood, my lord?
Or to the dreadful summit of the cliff
That beetles o'er his base into the sea,
And there assume some other horrible form
75 Which might deprive your sovereignty of reason
And draw you into madness? Think of it.
The very place puts toys of desperation,
Without more motive, into every brain
That looks so many fathoms to the sea
80 And hears it roar beneath.

Hamlet. It waves me still.—Go on, I'll follow thee.

Marcellus. You shall not go, my lord.

[*They hold back* Hamlet.]

Hamlet.   Hold off your hands.

Horatio. Be ruled. You shall not go.

Hamlet.   My fate cries out
And makes each petty arture in this body
85 As hardy as the Nemean lion's nerve.
Still am I called. Unhand me, gentlemen.
By heaven, I'll make a ghost of him that lets me!
I say, away!—Go on. I'll follow thee.

[Ghost *and* Hamlet *exit.*]

Horatio. He waxes desperate with imagination.

90 **Marcellus.** Let's follow. 'Tis not fit thus to obey him.

Horatio. Have after. To what issue will this come?

7 **bound:** obligated.

Marcellus. Something is rotten in the state of Denmark.

Horatio. Heaven will direct it.

Marcellus.   Nay, let's follow him.

[*They exit.*]

Scene 5 *Another part of the fortifications.*

The Ghost identifies itself as the spirit of Hamlet's father and reveals that he was murdered by Claudius. After describing this crime in horrible detail, the Ghost demands that Hamlet avenge the murder. Hamlet vows to carry out his father's wishes. He makes Horatio and Marcellus, who have followed him, swear to reveal nothing about what they have seen.

[*Enter* Ghost *and* Hamlet.]

Hamlet. Whither wilt thou lead me? Speak. I'll go no
   further.

Ghost. Mark me.

Hamlet.   I will.

Ghost.   My hour is almost come
   When I to sulf'rous and tormenting flames
   Must render up myself.

Hamlet.   Alas, poor ghost!

5 **Ghost.** Pity me not, but lend thy serious hearing
   To what I shall unfold.

Hamlet. Speak. I am bound to hear.

Ghost. So art thou to revenge, when thou shalt hear.

Hamlet. What?

10 **Ghost.** I am thy father's spirit,
   Doomed for a certain term to walk the night

13 *crimes:* sins.

17 *harrow up:* tear up, disturb.

18 *Make . . . spheres:* make your two eyes like stars jump from their assigned places in the universe.

19 *knotted . . . locks:* carefully arranged hair.

20 *an end:* on end.

21 *fearful porpentine:* frightened porcupine.

22–23 The Ghost says he must not describe life beyond death to a living person.

28 *as . . . is:* which murder in general (*it*) is at the very least.

32–35 *I find . . . this:* I think you are willing, and you would have to be duller than the thick weed that grows on the banks of Lethe (the river of forgetfulness in the underworld) to not be roused by this.

36 *orchard:* garden.

37–39 *So . . . abused:* Thus all of Denmark is utterly deceived by a false account of my death.

43 *adulterate:* adulterous.

And for the day confined to fast in fires
Till the foul crimes done in my days of nature
Are burnt and purged away. But that I am forbid
15   To tell the secrets of my prison house,
I could a tale unfold whose lightest word
Would harrow up thy soul, freeze thy young blood,
Make thy two eyes, like stars, start from their spheres,
Thy knotted and combinèd locks to part,
20   And each particular hair to stand an end,
Like quills upon the fearful porpentine.
But this eternal blazon must not be
To ears of flesh and blood. List, list, O list!
If thou didst ever thy dear father love—

25 **Hamlet.** O God!

Ghost. Revenge his foul and most unnatural murder.

Hamlet. Murder?

Ghost. Murder most foul, as in the best it is,
But this most foul, strange, and unnatural.

30 **Hamlet.** Haste me to know 't, that I, with wings as swift
As meditation or the thoughts of love,
May sweep to my revenge.

Ghost.   I find thee apt;
And duller shouldst thou be than the fat weed
That roots itself in ease on Lethe wharf,
35   Wouldst thou not stir in this. Now, Hamlet, hear.
'Tis given out that, sleeping in my orchard,
A serpent stung me. So the whole ear of Denmark
Is by a forgèd process of my death
Rankly abused. But know, thou noble youth,
40   The serpent that did sting thy father's life
Now wears his crown.

Hamlet. O, my prophetic soul! My uncle!

Ghost. Ay, that incestuous, that adulterate beast,
With witchcraft of his wit, with traitorous gifts—

54–58 The Ghost compares virtue, which remains pure even if indecency courts it in a heavenly form, with lust, which will grow weary of a virtuous marriage and seek pleasure in depravity.

63 *hebona:* a poisonous plant.

64 *porches:* entrances.

65 *leprous distilment:* a distilled liquid that causes disfigurement similar to that caused by leprosy.

69–71 *doth . . . blood:* The poison curdles the blood like something sour dropped into milk.

72–74 *most instant . . . body:* An eruption of sores (**tetter**) instantly covered my smooth body, leper-like (**lazar-like**), with a vile crust like the bark on a tree.

76 *dispatched:* deprived.

77–80 The Ghost regrets that he had no chance to receive the last rites of the church; he died with all his sins unabsolved.

45 O wicked wit and gifts, that have the power
So to seduce!—won to his shameful lust
The will of my most seeming-virtuous queen.
O Hamlet, what a falling off was there!
From me, whose love was of that dignity
50 That it went hand in hand even with the vow
I made to her in marriage, and to decline
Upon a wretch whose natural gifts were poor
To those of mine.
But virtue, as it never will be moved,
55 Though lewdness court it in a shape of heaven,
So, lust, though to a radiant angel linked,
Will sate itself in a celestial bed
And prey on garbage.
But soft, methinks I scent the morning air.
60 Brief let me be. Sleeping within my orchard,
My custom always of the afternoon,
Upon my secure hour thy uncle stole,
With juice of curséd hebona in a vial,
And in the porches of my ears did pour
65 The leprous distilment, whose effect
Holds such an enmity with blood of man
That swift as quicksilver it courses through
The natural gates and alleys of the body,
And with a sudden vigor it doth posset
70 And curd, like eager droppings into milk,
The thin and wholesome blood. So did it mine,
And a most instant tetter barked about,
Most lazar-like, with vile and loathsome crust
All my smooth body.
75 Thus was I, sleeping, by a brother's hand
Of life, of crown, of queen at once dispatched,
Cut off, even in the blossoms of my sin,
Unhouseled, disappointed, unaneled,
No reck'ning made, but sent to my account
80 With all my imperfections on my head.
O horrible, O horrible, most horrible!
If thou hast nature in thee, bear it not.

84 *luxury:* lust.

86–89 The Ghost tells Hamlet not to think of revenge against his mother.

90 *matin:* morning.

94 *couple:* add.

98 *globe:* head.

99–105 Hamlet vows to erase from the slate (*table*) of his memory all foolish notes (*fond records*), wise sayings (*saws*) he copied from books, and past impressions (*pressures past*) so that the Ghost's command will live in his mind unmixed with ordinary, insignificant thoughts.

Let not the royal bed of Denmark be
A couch for luxury and damnèd incest.
85 But, howsomever thou pursues this act,
Taint not thy mind, nor let thy soul contrive
Against thy mother aught. Leave her to heaven
And to those thorns that in her bosom lodge
To prick and sting her. Fare thee well at once.
90 The glowworm shows the matin to be near
And 'gins to pale his uneffectual fire.
Adieu, adieu, adieu. Remember me.

[*He exits.*]

Hamlet. O all you host of heaven! O earth! What else?
And shall I couple hell? O fie! Hold, hold, my heart,
95 And you, my sinews, grow not instant old,
But bear me stiffly up. Remember thee?
Ay, thou poor ghost, whiles memory holds a seat
In this distracted globe. Remember thee?
Yea, from the table of my memory
100 I'll wipe away all trivial, fond records,
All saws of books, all forms, all pressures past,
That youth and observation copied there,
And thy commandment all alone shall live
Within the book and volume of my brain,
105 Unmixed with baser matter. Yes, by heaven!
O most pernicious woman!
O villain, villain, smiling, damnèd villain!
My tables—meet it is I set it down
That one may smile and smile and be a villain.
110 At least I am sure it may be so in Denmark.

[*He writes.*]

So, uncle, there you are. Now to my word.
It is "adieu, adieu, remember me."
I have sworn 't.

[*Enter* Horatio *and* Marcellus.]

Horatio. My lord, my lord!

119 Hamlet responds to Marcellus's greeting (***Illo, ho,ho***) with the call of a falconer to his hawk.

128 *arrant knave:* thoroughly dishonest person.

131 *circumstance:* elaboration.

Marcellus. Lord Hamlet.

Horatio. Heavens secure him!

Hamlet. So be it.

Marcellus. Illo, ho, ho, my lord!

Hamlet. Hillo, ho, ho, boy! Come, bird, come!

Marcellus. How is 't, my noble lord?

Horatio. What news, my lord?

Hamlet. O, wonderful!

Horatio. Good my lord, tell it.

Hamlet. No, you will reveal it.

Horatio. Not I, my lord, by heaven.

Marcellus. Nor I, my lord.

Hamlet. How say you, then? Would heart of man once
   think it?

But you'll be secret?

Horatio/Marcellus. Ay, by heaven, my lord.

Hamlet. There's never a villain dwelling in all Denmark
   But he's an arrant knave.

Horatio. There needs no ghost, my lord, come from
   the grave
To tell us this.

Hamlet. Why, right, you are in the right.
   And so, without more circumstance at all,
   I hold it fit that we shake hands and part,
   You, as your business and desire shall point you
   (For every man hath business and desire,
   Such as it is), and for my own poor part,
   I will go pray.

Horatio. These are but wild and whirling words, my lord.

142 *honest:* genuine.

153 The hilt of a sword, shaped like a cross, was often used for swearing oaths.

156 *truepenny:* honest fellow.

162 *Hic et ubique:* here and everywhere (Latin).

Hamlet. I am sorry they offend you, heartily;
Yes, faith, heartily.

Horatio.   There's no offense, my lord.

140 **Hamlet.** Yes, by Saint Patrick, but there is, Horatio,
And much offense, too. Touching this vision here,
It is an honest ghost—that let me tell you.
For your desire to know what is between us,
O'ermaster 't as you may. And now, good friends,
145 As you are friends, scholars, and soldiers,
Give me one poor request.

Horatio. What is 't, my lord? We will.

Hamlet. Never make known what you have seen tonight.

Horatio/Marcellus. My lord, we will not.

150 **Hamlet.** Nay, but swear 't.

Horatio. In faith, my lord, not I.

Marcellus. Nor I, my lord, in faith.

Hamlet. Upon my sword.

Marcellus.   We have sworn, my lord, already.

Hamlet. Indeed, upon my sword, indeed.

155 **Ghost** [*cries under the stage*]. Swear.

Hamlet. Ha, ha, boy, sayst thou so? Art thou there,
truepenny?
Come on, you hear this fellow in the cellarage.
Consent to swear.

Horatio.   Propose the oath, my lord.

Hamlet. Never to speak of this that you have seen,
160 Swear by my sword.

Ghost [*beneath*]. Swear.

Hamlet. *Hic et ubique?* Then we'll shift our ground.
Come hither, gentlemen,

169 *pioner:* digger, miner.

171 Hamlet tells Horatio to welcome, or accept, the night's events as one would welcome a stranger.

173 *your philosophy:* the general subject of philosophy (not a particular belief of Horatio's).

174–185 Hamlet reveals that he may have to disguise himself with strange behavior (*antic disposition*); he has them swear not to make any gestures or hints that would give him away.

188–191 Hamlet says that he entrusts himself to them and will do his best to reward them.

193 *The . . . joint:* Everything is in disorder.

And lay your hands again upon my sword.
165 Swear by my sword
Never to speak of this that you have heard.

Ghost [*beneath*].Swear by his sword.

Hamlet. Well said, old mole. Canst work i' th' earth so
fast?
A worthy pioner! Once more remove, good friends.

170 **Horatio.** O day and night, but this is wondrous strange.

Hamlet. And therefore as a stranger give it welcome.
There are more things in heaven and earth, Horatio,
Than are dreamt of in your philosophy. But come.
Here, as before, never, so help you mercy,
175 How strange or odd some'er I bear myself
(As I perchance hereafter shall think meet
To put an antic disposition on)
That you, at such times seeing me, never shall,
With arms encumbered thus, or this headshake,
180 Or by pronouncing of some doubtful phrase,
As "Well, well, we know," or "We could an if we
would,"
Or "If we list to speak," or "There be an if they
might,"
Or such ambiguous giving-out, to note
That you know aught of me—this do swear,
185 So grace and mercy at your most need help you.

Ghost [*beneath*]. Swear.

Hamlet. Rest, rest, perturbèd spirit.—So, gentlemen,
With all my love I do commend me to you,
And what so poor a man as Hamlet is
190 May do t' express his love and friending to you,
God willing, shall not lack. Let us go in together,
And still your fingers on your lips, I pray.
The time is out of joint. O cursèd spite
That ever I was born to set it right!
195 Nay, come, let's go together.

[*They exit.*]

4 *make inquire:* ask questions.

6–12 Polonius tells him to start by asking which Danes (***Danskers***) are in Paris, how much money they have, where they live (***keep***), and other general questions, because he will find out more through this roundabout approach (***encompassment***) than by asking specific questions about Laertes.

13 *Take you:* assume.

ACT **TWO**

Scene 1 *Polonius's chambers.*

Polonius sends his servant to spy on Laertes in Paris.
Ophelia enters the room. She describes a frightening visit
from Hamlet, who behaved as if he were insane.
Polonius, assuming that Hamlet has been driven mad by
love, takes Ophelia to tell her story to Claudius.

[*Enter old* Polonius *with his man* Reynaldo.]

Polonius. Give him this money and these notes,
    Reynaldo.

Reynaldo. I will, my lord.

Polonius. You shall do marvelous wisely, good
    Reynaldo,
  Before you visit him, to make inquire
5 Of his behavior.

Reynaldo.   My lord, I did intend it.

Polonius. Marry, well said, very well said. Look you, sir,
  Inquire me first what Danskers are in Paris;
  And how, and who, what means, and where they
    keep,
  What company, at what expense; and finding
10 By this encompassment and drift of question
  That they do know my son, come you more nearer
  Than your particular demands will touch it.
  Take you, as 'twere, some distant knowledge of him,
  As thus: "I know his father and his friends
15 And, in part, him." Do you mark this, Reynaldo?

19–20 ***put on . . . please:*** accuse him of whatever faults you wish to make up; ***rank:*** gross.

22 ***wanton:*** reckless.

23–24 ***As are . . . liberty:*** that are commonly associated with youth and freedom.

24 ***gaming:*** gambling.

26 ***drabbing:*** going to prostitutes.

28 ***you . . . charge:*** You can soften (***season***) the charge by the way you state it.

30 ***incontinency:*** habitual sexual misconduct (as opposed to an occasional lapse).

31–36 Polonius tells him to describe Laertes's faults so subtly (***quaintly***) that they will seem the faults that come with independence (***taints of liberty***), the sudden urges of an excited mind, a wildness in untamed (***unreclaimèd***) blood that occurs in most men.

37 ***Wherefore:*** why.

40 ***fetch of wit:*** clever move.

41–46 Polonius wants Reynaldo to put these small stains (***sullies***) on his son's reputation—similar to the way in which cloth might be dirtied when it is handled—and then ask the person whether he has seen Laertes engaged in the offenses Reynaldo has mentioned (***prenominate crimes***).

Reynaldo. Ay, very well, my lord.

Polonius. "And, in part, him, but," you may say, "not
    well.
    But if 't be he I mean, he's very wild,
    Addicted so and so." And there put on him
20   What forgeries you please—marry, none so rank
    As may dishonor him, take heed of that,
    But, sir, such wanton, wild, and usual slips
    As are companions noted and most known
    To youth and liberty.

Reynaldo.   As gaming, my lord.

25 **Polonius.** Ay, or drinking, fencing, swearing,
    Quarreling, drabbing—you may go so far.

Reynaldo. My lord, that would dishonor him.

Polonius. Faith, no, as you may season it in the charge.
    You must not put another scandal on him
30   That he is open to incontinency;
    That's not my meaning. But breathe his faults so
      quaintly
    That they may seem the taints of liberty,
    The flash and outbreak of a fiery mind,
    A savageness in unreclaimèd blood,
35   Of general assault.

Reynaldo. But, my good lord—

Polonius. Wherefore should you do this?

Reynaldo. Ay, my lord, I would know that.

Polonius. Marry, sir, here's my drift,
40   And I believe it is a fetch of wit.
    You, laying these slight sullies on my son,
    As 'twere a thing a little soiled i' th' working,
    Mark you, your party in converse, him you would
      sound,
    Having ever seen in the prenominate crimes
45   The youth you breathe of guilty, be assured

46 *He closes . . . consequence:* he agrees with you in the following way.

48 *addition:* form of address.

59 *o'ertook in 's rouse:* overcome by drink.

62 *Videlicet:* namely.

64–66 *we of . . . out:* we who have wisdom and intelligence (*reach*) find things out indirectly, through roundabout courses (*windlasses*) and indirect tests (*assays of bias*). *How would you describe Polonius as a father?*

71–73 Polonius tells him to observe Laertes's behavior personally and to see that Laertes practices his music.

He closes with you in this consequence:
"Good sir," or so, or "friend," or "gentleman,"
According to the phrase or the addition
Of man and country—

Reynaldo.   Very good, my lord.

50 **Polonius.** And then, sir, does he this, he does—what was I
about to say? By the Mass, I was about to say something. Where did I leave?

Reynaldo. At "closes in the consequence," at "friend, or
so, and gentleman."

55 **Polonius.** At "closes in the consequence"—ay, marry—
He closes thus: "I know the gentleman.
I saw him yesterday," or "th' other day"
(Or then, or then, with such or such), "and as you say,
There was he gaming, there o'ertook in 's rouse,
60 There falling out at tennis"; or perchance
"I saw him enter such a house of sale"—
Videlicet, a brothel—or so forth. See you now
Your bait of falsehood take this carp of truth;
And thus do we of wisdom and of reach,
65 With windlasses and with assays of bias,
By indirections find directions out.
So by my former lecture and advice
Shall you my son. You have me, have you not?

Reynaldo. My lord, I have.

Polonius.   God be wi' you. Fare you well.

70 **Reynaldo.** Good my lord.

Polonius. Observe his inclination in yourself.

Reynaldo. I shall, my lord.

Polonius. And let him ply his music.

Reynaldo. Well, my lord.

75 **Polonius.**   Farewell.

78 *closet:* private room.

79 *doublet all unbraced:* jacket entirely unfastened.

80 *fouled:* dirty.

81 *down-gyvèd to his ankle:* fallen down to his ankles (like a prisoner's ankle chains, or gyves).

83 *purport:* expression.

96 *bulk:* body.

101 *to the last . . . me:* kept his eyes upon me the whole time.

103–107 Polonius says that the violent nature (**property**) of this love madness (**ecstasy**) often leads people to do something desperate.

[Reynaldo *exits*.]

[*Enter* Ophelia.]

How now, Ophelia, what's the matter?

Ophelia. O, my lord, my lord, I have been so affrighted!

Polonius. With what, i' th' name of God?

Ophelia. My lord, as I was sewing in my closet,
Lord Hamlet, with his doublet all unbraced,
80 No hat upon his head, his stockings fouled,
Ungartered, and down-gyvèd to his ankle,
Pale as his shirt, his knees knocking each other,
And with a look so piteous in purport
As if he had been loosèd out of hell
85 To speak of horrors—he comes before me.

Polonius. Mad for thy love?

Ophelia.   My lord, I do not know,
But truly I do fear it.

Polonius.   What said he?

Ophelia. He took me by the wrist and held me hard.
Then goes he to the length of all his arm,
90 And, with his other hand thus o'er his brow,
He falls to such perusal of my face
As he would draw it. Long stayed he so.
At last, a little shaking of mine arm,
And thrice his head thus waving up and down,
95 He raised a sigh so piteous and profound
As it did seem to shatter all his bulk
And end his being. That done, he lets me go,
And, with his head over his shoulder turned,
He seemed to find his way without his eyes,
100 For out o' doors he went without their helps
And to the last bended their light on me.

Polonius. Come, go with me. I will go seek the King.
This is the very ecstasy of love,

113 *coted:* observed.

114 *wrack:* ruin, seduce; ***beshrew my jealousy:*** curse my suspicious nature.

115–118 It is as natural for old people to go too far (***cast beyond ourselves***) with their suspicions as it is for younger people to lack good judgment.

119–120 Polonius decides that although it may anger the King, he must be told about this love because keeping it a secret might create even more grief.

Whose violent property fordoes itself
105 And leads the will to desperate undertakings
As oft as any passions under heaven
That does afflict our natures. I am sorry.
What, have you given him any hard words of late?

Ophelia. No, my good lord, but as you did command
110 I did repel his letters and denied
His access to me.

Polonius.   That hath made him mad.
I am sorry that with better heed and judgment
I had not coted him. I feared he did but trifle
And meant to wrack thee. But beshrew my jealousy!
115 By heaven, it is as proper to our age
To cast beyond ourselves in our opinions
As it is common for the younger sort
To lack discretion. Come, go we to the King.
This must be known, which, being kept close,
    might move
120 More grief to hide than hate to utter love.
Come.

[*They exit.*]

Scene 2 *The castle.*

*The King and Queen ask Rosencrantz and Guildenstern,
Hamlet's childhood friends, to find out why Hamlet is
behaving strangely. News that the ambassadors have
prevented Fortinbras from attacking Denmark is followed
by Polonius's claim that he has discovered the cause of
Hamlet's madness. Claudius agrees to test Polonius's
theory by eavesdropping on Hamlet while he talks to
Ophelia.*

*The King and Queen leave when Hamlet enters the room.
Hamlet is questioned by Polonius and later by
Rosencrantz and Guildenstern. He accuses his old friends*

6 ***Sith . . . man:*** since neither his appearance nor his personality.

10–18 Because Rosencrantz and Guildenstern were childhood friends with Hamlet and are so familiar with his past and his usual manner (***havior***), Claudius asks them to agree to stay (***vouchsafe your rest***) at court awhile to cheer Hamlet up and find out whether he is troubled by something that Claudius is unaware of. *Do you believe that Claudius has brought them to Elsinore because he wants to help Hamlet?*

18 ***opened:*** revealed.

22 ***gentry:*** courtesy.

24 ***For . . . hope:*** to aid and fulfill our wishes.

of being spies, but they distract him by announcing the arrival of a theater troupe. Hamlet welcomes the actors and asks them to perform a play at the castle. When he is alone, he contrasts his own silence and inaction with the rage shown by one of the actors while delivering a speech. He reveals that he will use the following night's performance to determine whether Claudius is guilty.

[*Flourish. Enter* King *and* Queen, Rosencrantz *and* Guildenstern *and* Attendants.]

King. Welcome, dear Rosencrantz and Guildenstern.
  Moreover that we much did long to see you,
  The need we have to use you did provoke
  Our hasty sending. Something have you heard
5 Of Hamlet's transformation, so call it,
  Sith nor th' exterior nor the inward man
  Resembles that it was. What it should be,
  More than his father's death, that thus hath put him
  So much from th' understanding of himself
10 I cannot dream of. I entreat you both
  That, being of so young days brought up with him
  And sith so neighbored to his youth and havior,
  That you vouchsafe your rest here in our court
  Some little time, so by your companies
15 To draw him on to pleasures, and to gather
  So much as from occasion you may glean,
  Whether aught to us unknown afflicts him thus
  That, opened, lies within our remedy.

Queen. Good gentlemen, he hath much talked of you,
20 And sure I am two men there is not living
  To whom he more adheres. If it will please you
  To show us so much gentry and goodwill
  As to expend your time with us awhile
  For the supply and profit of our hope,
25 Your visitation shall receive such thanks
  As fits a king's remembrance.

Rosencrantz.   Both your Majesties

29–32 Guildenstern promises that they will devote themselves entirely (*in the full bent*) to the service of the King and Queen.

38 *practices:* doings (sometimes used to mean "trickery").

42 *still:* always.

47–48 *Hunts . . . do:* does not follow the path of political shrewdness as well as it used to.

52 *fruit:* dessert.

Might, by the sovereign power you have of us,
Put your dread pleasures more into command
Than to entreaty.

Guildenstern.   But we both obey,
30   And here give up ourselves in the full bent
To lay our service freely at your feet,
To be commanded.

King. Thanks, Rosencrantz and gentle Guildenstern.

Queen. Thanks, Guildenstern and gentle Rosencrantz.
35   And I beseech you instantly to visit
My too much changèd son. Go, some of you,
And bring these gentlemen where Hamlet is.

Guildenstern. Heavens make our presence and our
      practices
Pleasant and helpful to him!

Queen.   Ay, amen!

[Rosencrantz *and* Guildenstern *exit with some* Attendants.]

[*Enter* Polonius.]

40 **Polonius.** Th' ambassadors from Norway, my good lord,
Are joyfully returned.

King. Thou still hast been the father of good news.

Polonius. Have I, my lord? I assure my good liege
I hold my duty as I hold my soul,
45   Both to my God and to my gracious king,
And I do think, or else this brain of mine
Hunts not the trail of policy so sure
As it hath used to do, that I have found
The very cause of Hamlet's lunacy.

50 **King.** O, speak of that! That do I long to hear.

Polonius. Give first admittance to th' ambassadors.
My news shall be the fruit to that great feast.

King. Thyself do grace to them and bring them in.

56 *the main:* the main matter.

58 *sift him:* question Polonius carefully.

59 *brother:* fellow king.

61 *Upon our first:* as soon as we brought up the matter.

67 *borne in hand:* deceived; *arrests:* orders to desist.

69 *in fine:* finally.

71 *give . . . against:* challenge militarily.

77–80 *give . . . down:* allow troops to move through Denmark for this expedition, under the conditions set down for Denmark's security and Fortinbras's permission.

[Polonius *exits.*]

He tells me, my dear Gertrude, he hath found
55 The head and source of all your son's distemper.

Queen. I doubt it is no other but the main—
His father's death and our o'erhasty marriage.

King. Well, we shall sift him.

[*Enter* Ambassadors Voltemand *and* Cornelius *with* Polonius.]

Welcome, my good friends.
Say, Voltemand, what from our brother Norway?

60 **Voltemand.** Most fair return of greetings and desires.
Upon our first, he sent out to suppress
His nephew's levies, which to him appeared
To be a preparation 'gainst the Polack,
But, better looked into, he truly found
65 It was against your Highness. Whereat, grieved
That so his sickness, age, and impotence
Was falsely borne in hand, sends out arrests
On Fortinbras, which he, in brief, obeys,
Receives rebuke from Norway, and, in fine,
70 Makes vow before his uncle never more
To give th' assay of arms against your Majesty.
Whereon old Norway, overcome with joy,
Gives him three-score thousand crowns in annual
fee
And his commission to employ those soldiers,
75 So levied as before, against the Polack,
With an entreaty, herein further shown,

[*He gives a paper.*]

That it might please you to give quiet pass
Through your dominions for this enterprise,
On such regards of safety and allowance
80 As therein are set down.

80 *likes:* pleases.

81 *our more considered time:* a more suitable time for consideration.

86–89 To inquire into (**expostulate**) the nature of one's duty to the crown would be a waste of time, like trying to figure out the reason for day, night, and time.

90 *brevity . . . wit:* intelligent speech should be concise.

91 *flourishes:* decorations.

96–99 The Queen asks Polonius to make his point without such a display of rhetoric (**art**). He claims to be speaking plainly about the matter, but then he can't resist making a figure of speech that even he describes as foolish.

105 *Perpend:* consider.

108 *gather and surmise:* draw your own conclusions.

King.   It likes us well,
And, at our more considered time, we'll read,
Answer, and think upon this business.
Meantime, we thank you for your well-took labor.
Go to your rest. At night we'll feast together.
85   Most welcome home!

[Voltemand *and* Cornelius *exit.*]

Polonius.   This business is well ended.
My liege, and madam, to expostulate
What majesty should be, what duty is,
Why day is day, night night, and time is time
Were nothing but to waste night, day, and time.
90   Therefore, since brevity is the soul of wit,
And tediousness the limbs and outward flourishes,
I will be brief. Your noble son is mad.
"Mad" call I it, for, to define true madness,
What is 't but to be nothing else but mad?
95   But let that go.

Queen.   More matter with less art.

Polonius. Madam, I swear I use no art at all.
That he's mad, 'tis true; 'tis true 'tis pity,
And pity 'tis 'tis true—a foolish figure,
But farewell it, for I will use no art.
100   Mad let us grant him then, and now remains
That we find out the cause of this effect,
Or, rather say, the cause of this defect,
For this effect defective comes by cause.
Thus it remains, and the remainder thus.
105   Perpend.
I have a daughter (have while she is mine)
Who, in her duty and obedience, mark,
Hath given me this. Now gather and surmise.

[*He reads.*] *To the celestial, and my soul's idol, the*
110   *most beautified Ophelia*—

That's an ill phrase, a vile phrase; "beautified" is a

114–115 The Queen seems doubtful that Hamlet would use such formal and flowery language; Polonius asks her to wait and assures her that he will read the letter accurately.

116 *Doubt:* suspect.

120 *ill at these numbers:* bad at writing in verse.
121 *reckon:* count, put into metrical verse.

123–124 *whilst . . . to him:* while I am still in this body (*machine*).

126–128 *more above . . . ear:* In addition, she has told me all the details of his solicitations as they occurred (*fell out*).

137 *played . . . table-book:* kept this knowledge hidden within me.
138 *given . . . winking:* closed the eyes of my heart.
139 *with idle sight:* saw without really noticing.

142 *star:* sphere.
143 *prescripts:* orders.

vile phrase. But you shall hear. Thus: [*He reads.*]
In her excellent white bosom, these, etc.—

Queen. Came this from Hamlet to her?

115 **Polonius.** Good madam, stay awhile. I will be faithful.

[*He reads the letter.*]

> *Doubt thou the stars are fire,*
> > *Doubt that the sun doth move,*
> *Doubt truth to be a liar,*
> > *But never doubt I love.*

120 *O dear Ophelia, I am ill at these numbers. I have not*
art to reckon my groans, but that I love thee
best, O most best, believe it. Adieu.
> > > *Thine evermore, most dear lady, whilst*
> > > > *this machine is to him, Hamlet.*

125 This, in obedience, hath my daughter shown me,
And more above, hath his solicitings,
As they fell out by time, by means, and place,
All given to mine ear.

King. But how hath she received his love?

130 **Polonius.** What do you think of me?

King. As of a man faithful and honorable.

Polonius. I would fain prove so. But what might you
   think,
When I had seen this hot love on the wing
(As I perceived it, I must tell you that,
135 Before my daughter told me), what might you,
Or my dear Majesty your queen here, think,
If I had played the desk or table-book
Or given my heart a winking, mute and dumb,
Or looked upon this love with idle sight?
140 What might you think? No, I went round to work,
And my young mistress thus I did bespeak:
"Lord Hamlet is a prince, out of thy star.
This must not be." And then I prescripts gave her,

144 *resort:* visits.

147–152 Polonius describes the stages of Hamlet's decline
(***declension***): he grew sad, then stopped eating (***a***
fast), then suffered from sleeplessness (***a watch***), then
turned weak and light-headed, and finally became
mad.

157 The actor playing Polonius might point from his head to
his shoulder or make a similar gesture while speaking
this line.

160 ***the center:*** the Earth's center, the most inaccessible
place; ***try:*** test.

163 ***loose:*** turn loose (as an animal might be released for
mating).

164 ***arras:*** a tapestry hung in front of a wall.

That she should lock herself from his resort,
145 Admit no messengers, receive no tokens;
Which done, she took the fruits of my advice,
And he, repelled (a short tale to make),
Fell into a sadness, then into a fast,
Thence to a watch, thence into a weakness,
150 Thence to a lightness, and, by this declension,
Into the madness wherein now he raves
And all we mourn for.

King. [*to* Queen].   Do you think 'tis this?

Queen. It may be, very like.

Polonius. Hath there been such a time (I would fain
know that)
155 That I have positively said "'Tis so,"
When it proved otherwise?

King.   Not that I know.

Polonius. Take this from this, if this be otherwise.
If circumstances lead me, I will find
Where truth is hid, though it were hid, indeed,
160 Within the center.

King.   How may we try it further?

Polonius. You know sometimes he walks four hours
together
Here in the lobby.

Queen.   So he does indeed.

Polonius. At such a time I'll loose my daughter to him.
[*To the King.*] Be you and I behind an arras then.
165 Mark the encounter. If he love her not,
And be not from his reason fall'n thereon,
Let me be no assistant for a state,
But keep a farm and carters.

King.   We will try it.

[*Enter* Hamlet *reading on a book.*]

171 *board him presently:* speak to him at once.

175 *fishmonger:* fish seller.

183 *a good kissing carrion:* good flesh for kissing. (Hamlet seems to be reading at least part of this sentence from his book.)

185 *Conception:* understanding, being pregnant.

188 *harping on:* sticking to the subject of.

195 *matter:* subject matter. (Hamlet plays off another meaning, "the basis of a quarrel.")

Queen. But look where sadly the poor wretch comes
    reading.

170 **Polonius.** Away, I do beseech you both, away.
    I'll board him presently. O, give me leave.

[King *and* Queen *exit with* Attendants.]

How does my good Lord Hamlet?

Hamlet. Well, God-a-mercy.

Polonius. Do you know me, my lord?

175 **Hamlet.** Excellent well. You are a fishmonger.

Polonius. Not I, my lord.

Hamlet. Then I would you were so honest a man.

Polonius. Honest, my lord?

Hamlet. Ay, sir. To be honest, as this world goes, is to
180   be one man picked out of ten thousand.

Polonius. That's very true, my lord.

Hamlet. For if the sun breed maggots in a dead dog,
    being a good kissing carrion—Have you a daughter?

Polonius. I have, my lord.

185 **Hamlet.** Let her not walk i' th' sun. Conception is a
    blessing, but, as your daughter may conceive,
    friend, look to 't.

Polonius [*aside*]. How say you by that? Still harping on
    my daughter. Yet he knew me not at first; he said I
190   was a fishmonger. He is far gone. And truly, in my
    youth, I suffered much extremity for love, very
    near this. I'll speak to him again.—What do you
    read, my lord?

Hamlet. Words, words, words.

195 **Polonius.** What is the matter, my lord?

201 *wit:* understanding.

204 *honesty:* good manners.

208 Polonius asks him to come out of the open air.

211 *pregnant:* full of meaning; *happiness:* talent for expression.

Hamlet. Between who?

Polonius. I mean the matter that you read, my lord.

Hamlet. Slanders, sir; for the satirical rogue says here
that old men have gray beards, that their faces are
200 wrinkled, their eyes purging thick amber and plum-
tree gum, and that they have a plentiful lack of wit,
together with most weak hams; all which, sir,
though I most powerfully and potently believe, yet
I hold it not honesty to have it thus set down; for
205 yourself, sir, shall grow old as I am, if, like a crab,
you could go backward.

Polonius [*aside*]. Though this be madness, yet there is
method in 't.—Will you walk out of the air, my lord?

Hamlet. Into my grave?

210 **Polonius.** Indeed, that's out of the air. [*Aside.*] How
pregnant sometimes his replies are! A happiness that
often madness hits on, which reason and sanity
could not so prosperously be delivered of. I will
leave him and suddenly contrive the means of
215 meeting between him and my daughter.—My lord,
I will take my leave of you.

Hamlet. You cannot, sir, take from me anything that I
will more willingly part withal—except my life,
except my life, except my life.

220 **Polonius.** Fare you well, my lord.

Hamlet [*aside*]. These tedious old fools.

[*Enter* Guildenstern *and* Rosencrantz.]

Polonius. You go to seek the Lord Hamlet. There he is.

Rosencrantz [*to* Polonius]. God save you, sir.

[Polonius *exits.*]

Guildenstern. My honored lord.

229 *indifferent:* ordinary.

234–238 Hamlet exchanges sexual puns with his childhood friends. References to Fortune's sexual favors and private parts lead up to the traditional saying that the unfaithful Fortune is a prostitute (***strumpet***).

249 *confines:* places of confinement; ***wards:*** cells.

Rosencrantz. My most dear lord.

Hamlet. My excellent good friends! How dost thou, Guildenstern? Ah, Rosencrantz! Good lads, how do you both?

Rosencrantz. As the indifferent children of the earth.

Guildenstern. Happy in that we are not overhappy. On Fortune's cap, we are not the very button.

Hamlet. Nor the soles of her shoe?

Rosencrantz. Neither, my lord.

Hamlet. Then you live about her waist, or in the middle of her favors?

Guildenstern. Faith, her privates we.

Hamlet. In the secret parts of Fortune? O, most true! She is a strumpet. What news?

Rosencrantz. None, my lord, but that the world's grown honest.

Hamlet. Then is doomsday near. But your news is not true. Let me question more in particular. What have you, my good friends, deserved at the hands of Fortune that she sends you to prison hither?

Guildenstern. Prison, my lord?

Hamlet. Denmark's a prison.

Rosencrantz. Then is the world one.

Hamlet. A goodly one, in which there are many confines, wards, and dungeons, Denmark being one o' th' worst.

Rosencrantz. We think not so, my lord.

Hamlet. Why, then, 'tis none to you, for there is nothing either good or bad but thinking makes it so. To me, it is a prison.

260–262 Guildenstern remarks that the apparently substantial aims of ambition are even less substantial than dreams. *What kind of response from Hamlet might Guildenstern and Rosencrantz be seeking by raising the subject of ambition?*

266–267 Hamlet says that according to their logic, only beggars would have real bodies (since they lack ambition), and monarchs and ambitious (***outstretched***) heroes would be the shadows of beggars.

268 *fay:* faith.

269 *wait upon:* escort. (Hamlet takes the word to mean "serve" and replies that he would not categorize them with his servants.)

278 *too dear a halfpenny:* too costly at a halfpenny.

279 *free:* voluntary.

282 Hamlet sarcastically asks them to give him anything but a straight answer.

285 *color:* disguise.

255 **Rosencrantz.** Why, then, your ambition makes it one. 'Tis too narrow for your mind.

Hamlet. O God, I could be bounded in a nutshell and count myself a king of infinite space, were it not that I have bad dreams.

260 **Guildenstern.** Which dreams, indeed, are ambition, for the very substance of the ambitious is merely the shadow of a dream.

Hamlet. A dream itself is but a shadow.

Rosencrantz. Truly, and I hold ambition of so airy and
265 light a quality that it is but a shadow's shadow.

Hamlet. Then are our beggars bodies, and our monarchs and outstretched heroes the beggars' shadows. Shall we to th' court? For, by my fay, I cannot reason.

Rosencrantz/Guildenstern. We'll wait upon you.

270 **Hamlet.** No such matter. I will not sort you with the rest of my servants, for, to speak to you like an honest man, I am most dreadfully attended. But, in the beaten way of friendship, what make you at Elsinore?

275 **Rosencrantz.** To visit you, my lord, no other occasion.

Hamlet. Beggar that I am, I am even poor in thanks; but I thank you, and sure, dear friends, my thanks are too dear a halfpenny. Were you not sent for? Is it your own inclining? Is it a free visitation? Come,
280 come, deal justly with me. Come, come; nay, speak.

Guildenstern. What should we say, my lord?

Hamlet. Anything but to th' purpose. You were sent for, and there is a kind of confession in your looks which your modesties have not craft
285 enough to color. I know the good king and queen have sent for you.

288–289 *conjure you:* ask you earnestly.

289–290 *consonancy of our youth:* our closeness when we were young.

291–292 *by what . . . withal:* by whatever you hold more valuable, which someone more skillful than me would use to urge you with.

295–296 Hamlet reminds them that he is watching; he pleads with them not to hold back.

298–299 *shall my . . . discovery:* My saying it first will spare you from revealing your secret.

300 *molt no feather:* will not be diminished.

304 *promontory:* a rock jutting out from the sea.

305 *brave:* splendid, glorious.

306 *fretted:* adorned.

308 *congregation:* gathering.

309 *piece of work:* work of art or fine craftsmanship.

311 *express:* exact, expressive.

312 *apprehension:* understanding.

314 *quintessence of dust:* essence, or most refined form, of dust.

Rosencrantz. To what end, my lord?

Hamlet. That you must teach me. But let me conjure
you by the rights of our fellowship, by the conso-
290 nancy of our youth, by the obligation of our ever-
preserved love, and by what more dear a better
proposer can charge you withal: be even and
direct with me whether you were sent for or no.

Rosencrantz [*to* Guildenstern]. What say you?

295 **Hamlet** [*aside*]. Nay, then I have an eye of you.—If you
love me, hold not off.

Guildenstern. My lord, we were sent for.

Hamlet. I will tell you why; so shall my anticipation
prevent your discovery, and your secrecy to the
300 King and Queen molt no feather. I have of late,
but wherefore I know not, lost all my mirth, for-
gone all custom of exercises, and, indeed, it goes so
heavily with my disposition that this goodly frame,
the earth, seems to me a sterile promontory; this
305 most excellent canopy, the air, look you, this brave
o'er-hanging firmament, this majestical roof, fretted
with golden fire—why, it appeareth nothing to me
but a foul and pestilent congregation of vapors.
What a piece of work is a man, how noble in rea-
310 son, how infinite in faculties, in form and moving
how express and admirable; in action how like an
angel, in apprehension how like a god: the beauty
of the world, the paragon of animals—and yet, to
me, what is this quintessence of dust? Man delights
315 not me, no, nor women neither, though by your
smiling you seem to say so.

Rosencrantz. My lord, there was no such stuff in my
thoughts.

Hamlet. Why did you laugh, then, when I said "man
320 delights not me"?

322 *Lenten entertainment:* meager, or spare, reception.

323 *coted:* passed.

325–332 Hamlet anticipates the various stock characters to be played by the actors: the king shall receive his praise (*have tribute on me*), the knight shall use his sword and shield (*foil and target*), the lover shall not sigh for nothing (*gratis*), the eccentric (*humorous)* character shall play his part in peace (a role that is usually exaggerated and extreme, because the eccentric is dominated by one character trait), the clown shall make those laugh who do so easily (a *sear* is part of a gunlock), and the lady shall speak without restraint, or else the blank verse (which has five metrical feet) will limp (*halt*) because of it.

335–336 *Their . . . ways:* Remaining in the city would have added more to their reputation and profits.

337–349 The players have left the city because of a ban on their playing there (*inhibition*) due to a recent change (*late innovation*). Their fame has been eclipsed by a company of boy actors—a nest (*aerie*) of young hawks (*little eyases*) who are loudly applauded (*tyrannically clapped*) for their shrill performances. Many fashionable patrons are afraid to attend the public theaters (*common stages*) where adult actors play, fearing satirical attacks from the pens of those who write for the boy actors. (This description clearly alludes to a company of boy actors that became very popular in London shortly before *Hamlet* was written.)

351 *escoted:* provided for.

351–352 *pursue . . . sing:* follow the profession only until their voices change.

353 *common:* adult.

Rosencrantz. To think, my lord, if you delight not in man, what Lenten entertainment the players shall receive from you. We coted them on the way, and hither are they coming to offer you service.

325 **Hamlet.** He that plays the king shall be welcome—his Majesty shall have tribute on me. The adventurous knight shall use his foil and target, the lover shall not sigh gratis, the humorous man shall end his part in peace, the clown shall make those laugh

330 whose lungs are tickle o' th' sear, and the lady shall say her mind freely, or the blank verse shall halt for 't. What players are they?

Rosencrantz. Even those you were wont to take such delight in, the tragedians of the city.

335 **Hamlet.** How chances it they travel? Their residence, both in reputation and profit, was better both ways.

Rosencrantz. I think their inhibition comes by the means of the late innovation.

Hamlet. Do they hold the same estimation they did

340 when I was in the city? Are they so followed?

Rosencrantz. No, indeed are they not.

Hamlet. How comes it? Do they grow rusty?

Rosencrantz. Nay, their endeavor keeps in the wonted pace. But there is, sir, an aerie of children, little

345 eyases, that cry out on the top of question and are most tyrannically clapped for 't. These are now the fashion and so berattle the common stages (so they call them) that many wearing rapiers are afraid of goose quills and dare scarce come thither.

350 **Hamlet.** What, are they children? Who maintains 'em? How are they escoted? Will they pursue the quality no longer than they can sing? Will they not say afterwards, if they should grow themselves to common players (as it is most like, if their means are no bet-

356 *succession:* future work as actors.

358 *tar:* provoke.

359–361 ***There was . . . question:*** For a while the only profitable plays were satires that took part in the fierce rivalry between the boy company and the adult companies.

366–367 ***Ay . . . load:*** Yes, they've won over the whole theater world (Hercules carried the world on his shoulders for Atlas); possibly an allusion to the sign of the Globe Theatre, which pictured Hercules holding the world.

368–371 Hamlet says that people who made faces (***mouths***) at his uncle while his father was alive now pay up to 100 gold coins for his miniature portrait. *What do you think he is saying about Claudius in this statement?*

375–381 Hamlet tells Rosencrantz and Guildenstern that since fashion and ceremony should accompany a welcome, he wants to observe these formalities with the two of them so that it will not appear that the players get a better reception (***entertainment***) than they do.

384–385 Hamlet says he is only mad when the wind blows in a certain direction; at other times he can tell one thing from another. *Why do you think Hamlet makes this comment?*

355 ter), their writers do them wrong to make them
exclaim against their own succession?

Rosencrantz. Faith, there has been much to-do on
both sides, and the nation holds it no sin to tar
them to controversy. There was for a while no
360 money bid for argument unless the poet and the
player went to cuffs in the question.

Hamlet. Is 't possible?

Guildenstern. O, there has been much throwing about
of brains.

365 **Hamlet.** Do the boys carry it away?

Rosencrantz. Ay, that they do, my lord—Hercules and
his load too.

Hamlet. It is not very strange; for my uncle is King of
Denmark, and those that would make mouths at
370 him while my father lived give twenty, forty, fifty, a
hundred ducats apiece for his picture in little.
'Sblood, there is something in this more than natural, if philosophy could find it out.

[*A flourish for the* Players.]

Guildenstern. There are the players.

375 **Hamlet.** Gentlemen, you are welcome to Elsinore.
Your hands, come then. Th' appurtenance of welcome is fashion and ceremony. Let me comply with
you in this garb, lest my extent to the players,
which, I tell you, must show fairly outwards,
380 should more appear like entertainment than yours.
You are welcome. But my uncle-father and aunt-
mother are deceived.

Guildenstern. In what, my dear lord?

Hamlet. I am but mad north-north-west. When the
385 wind is southerly, I know a hawk from a handsaw.

389 *swaddling clouts:* cloth used to wrap a newborn baby.

397 *Roscius:* a famous Roman actor.

399 Hamlet dismisses the announcement as old news.

406 *Seneca:* a Roman writer of tragedies.

406–407 *Plautus:* a Roman writer of comedies; *For the . . . liberty:* for plays that follow strict rules of dramatic composition as well as more loosely written plays.

409–426 *Jephthah:* a biblical figure who sacrifices his beloved daughter after making a thoughtless vow (see Judges 11). Hamlet quotes lines from a ballad based on this story.

[*Enter* Polonius.]

Polonius. Well be with you, gentlemen.

Hamlet. Hark you, Guildenstern, and you too—at
each ear a hearer! That great baby you see there is
not yet out of his swaddling clouts.

390 **Rosencrantz.** Haply he is the second time come to
them, for they say an old man is twice a child.

Hamlet. I will prophesy he comes to tell me of the
players; mark it.—You say right, sir, a Monday
morning, 'twas then indeed.

395 **Polonius.** My lord, I have news to tell you.

Hamlet. My lord, I have news to tell you: when
Roscius was an actor in Rome—

Polonius. The actors are come hither, my lord.

Hamlet. Buzz, buzz.

400 **Polonius.** Upon my honor—

Hamlet. Then came each actor on his ass.

Polonius. The best actors in the world, either for
tragedy, comedy, history, pastoral, pastoral-
comical, historical-pastoral, tragical-historical,
405 tragical-comical-historical-pastoral, scene individ-
able, or poem unlimited. Seneca cannot be too
heavy, nor Plautus too light. For the law of writ
and the liberty, these are the only men.

Hamlet. O Jephthah, judge of Israel, what a treasure
410 hadst thou!

Polonius. What a treasure had he, my lord?

Hamlet. Why,
  One fair daughter, and no more,
  The which he lovèd passing well.

425 ***the first . . . chanson:*** the first stanza of the
religious song.

429 ***valanced:*** fringed (with a beard).

431–435 All female roles were played by boys. Hamlet fears that
this boy's voice might crack onstage, since he has
grown by the height of a thick-soled shoe (***altitude of
a chopine***).

436–437 ***fly . . . see:*** take on anything.

437 ***straight:*** right away.

444 ***caviary to the general:*** like caviar, which is unappreci-
ated by most people.

446 ***digested:*** arranged.

447 ***modesty:*** restraint

Polonius [*aside*]. Still on my daughter.

Hamlet. Am I not i' th' right, old Jephthah?

Polonius. If you call me "Jephthah," my lord: I have a
daughter that I love passing well.

Hamlet. Nay, that follows not.

420 **Polonius.** What follows then, my lord?

Hamlet. Why,
      As by lot, God wot
and then, you know,
      It came to pass, as most like it was—
425 the first row of the pious chanson will show you
more, for look where my abridgment comes.

[*Enter the* Players.]

You are welcome, masters; welcome all.—I am glad
to see thee well.—Welcome, good friends.—O my
old friend! Why, thy face is valanced since I saw
430 thee last. Com'st thou to beard me in Denmark?—
What, my young lady and mistress! By'r Lady,
your ladyship is nearer to heaven than when I saw
you last, by the altitude of a chopine. Pray God
your voice, like a piece of uncurrent gold, be not
435 cracked within the ring. Masters, you are all
welcome. We'll e'en to 't like French falconers, fly
at anything we see. We'll have a speech straight.
Come, give us a taste of your quality. Come, a passionate speech.

440 **First Player.** What speech, my good lord?

Hamlet. I heard thee speak me a speech once, but it
was never acted, or, if it was, not above once; for
the play, I remember, pleased not the million: 'twas
caviary to the general. But it was (as I received it,
445 and others whose judgments in such matters cried
in the top of mine) an excellent play, well digested
in the scenes, set down with as much modesty as

448 *cunning:* skill; *sallets:* spicy bits, racey jests.

454–455 Pyrrhus, son of the Greek hero Achilles, killed King Priam to revenge the death of his father during the Trojan War. Aeneas tells the story to Dido, the Queen of Carthage, in Virgil's *Aeneid.*

458 *Hyrcanian beast:* a tiger.

462 *couchèd:* concealed; *ominous horse:* wooden horse used by the Greeks to enter Troy.

465 *total gules:* all red; *tricked:* adorned.

467 The blood is baked and crusted (*impasted*) from the heat of the burning streets.

470 *o'ersizèd:* smeared over.
471 *carbuncles:* fiery red stones.

479 *Repugnant to:* resisting.

482 *unnervèd:* strengthless; *senseless Ilium:* the inanimate fortress of Troy.

cunning. I remember one said there were no sallets
in the lines to make the matter savory, nor no mat-
450 ter in the phrase that might indict the author of
affectation, but called it an honest method, as
wholesome as sweet and, by very much, more
handsome than fine. One speech in 't I chiefly
loved. 'Twas Aeneas' tale to Dido, and thereabout
455 of it especially when he speaks of Priam's slaughter.
If it live in your memory, begin at this line—let me
see, let me see:
The rugged Pyrrhus, like th' Hyrcanian beast—
'tis not so; it begins with Pyrrhus:
460 *The rugged Pyrrhus, he whose sable arms,*
Black as his purpose, did the night resemble
When he lay couchèd in th' ominous horse,
Hath now this dread and black complexion smeared
With heraldry more dismal. Head to foot,
465 *Now is he total gules, horridly tricked*
With blood of fathers, mothers, daughters, sons,
Baked and impasted with the parching streets,
That lend a tyrannous and a damnèd light
To their lord's murder. Roasted in wrath and fire,
470 *And thus o'ersizèd with coagulate gore,*
With eyes like carbuncles, the hellish Pyrrhus
Old grandsire Priam seeks.
So, proceed you.

Polonius. 'Fore God, my lord, well spoken, with good
475 accent and good discretion.

First Player.   *Anon he finds him*
Striking too short at Greeks. His antique sword,
Rebellious to his arm, lies where it falls,
Repugnant to command. Unequal matched,
480 *Pyrrhus at Priam drives, in rage strikes wide;*
But with the whiff and wind of his fell sword
Th' unnervèd father falls. Then senseless Ilium,
Seeming to feel this blow, with flaming top
Stoops to his base, and with a hideous crash

485 *Takes . . . ear:* captures Pyrrhus' attention.

488–490 *So . . . nothing:* Pyrrhus stood still like a tyrant in a painting, suspended between his intentions and taking the actions that would fulfill them.

492 *rack:* mass of high clouds.

497 *Cyclops:* one-eyed giants who worked for Vulcan, the Roman god of metalworking.

498 *Mars:* Roman god of war; *for proof eterne:* to last for eternity.

502 *synod:* assembly.

503 *fellies:* section of a wheel's rim.

504 *nave:* hub of a wheel.

508–509 *He's for . . . sleeps:* Unless he's hearing a comic song and dance (*jig*) or a bawdy tale, he falls asleep.

509 *Hecuba:* Priam's wife.

510 *moblèd:* her face was muffled.

514 *bisson rheum:* blinding tears; *clout:* cloth.

516 *o'erteemèd:* worn out from childbearing.

485 *Takes prisoner Pyrrhus' ear. For lo, his sword,*
Which was declining on the milky head
Of reverend Priam, seemed i' th' air to stick.
So as a painted tyrant Pyrrhus stood
And, like a neutral to his will and matter,
490 *Did nothing.*
But as we often see against some storm
A silence in the heavens, the rack stand still,
The bold winds speechless, and the orb below
As hush as death, anon the dreadful thunder
495 *Doth rend the region; so, after Pyrrhus' pause,*
Aroused vengeance sets him new a-work,
And never did the Cyclops' hammers fall
On Mars's armor, forged for proof eterne,
With less remorse than Pyrrhus' bleeding sword
500 *Now falls on Priam.*
Out, out, thou strumpet Fortune! All you gods
In general synod take away her power,
Break all the spokes and fellies from her wheel,
And bowl the round nave down the hill of heaven
505 *As low as to the fiends!*

Polonius. This is too long.

Hamlet. It shall to the barber's with your beard.—
Prithee say on. He's for a jig or a tale of bawdry, or
he sleeps. Say on; come to Hecuba.

510 **First Player.** *But who, ah woe, had seen the mobled*
queen—

Hamlet. "The mobled queen"?

Polonius. That's good. "Mobled queen" is good.

First Player. *Run barefoot up and down, threat'ning*
the flames
With bisson rheum, a clout upon that head
515 *Where late the diadem stood, and for a robe,*
About her lank and all o'erteemèd loins
A blanket, in the alarm of fear caught up—

519 *'Gainst . . . pronounced:* would have proclaimed treasonous statements against Fortune's rule.

525 *milch:* milky, moist with tears.

527 *whe'er:* whether.

532 *abstract:* summary.

537 *God's bodykins:* by God's little body.

548 *ha't:* have it.

Who this had seen, with tongue in venom steeped,
'Gainst Fortune's state would treason have pro-
    nounced.
520 *But if the gods themselves did see her then*
When she saw Pyrrhus make malicious sport
In mincing with his sword her husband's limbs,
The instant burst of clamor that she made
(Unless things mortal move them not at all)
525 *Would have made milch the burning eyes of heaven*
And passion in the gods.

Polonius. Look whe'er he has not turned his color and
has tears in 's eyes. Prithee, no more.

Hamlet. 'Tis well. I'll have thee speak out the rest of
530 this soon.—Good my lord, will you see the players
well bestowed? Do you hear, let them be well used,
for they are the abstract and brief chronicles of the
time. After your death you were better have a bad
epitaph than their ill report while you live.

535 **Polonius.** My lord, I will use them according to their
desert.

Hamlet. God's bodykins, man, much better! Use every
man after his desert and who shall 'scape whipping? Use them after your own honor and dignity.
540 The less they deserve, the more merit is in your
bounty. Take them in.

Polonius. Come, sirs.

Hamlet. Follow him, friends. We'll hear a play tomorrow. [*As* Polonius *and* Players *exit,* Hamlet *speaks to*
545 *the* First Player.] Dost thou hear me, old friend?
Can you play "The Murder of Gonzago"?

First Player. Ay, my lord.

Hamlet. We'll ha 't tomorrow night. You could, for a
need, study a speech of some dozen or sixteen
550 lines, which I would set down and insert in 't,

561–562 ***Could . . . wanned:*** could force his soul into such agreement with his thoughts that his soul made his face turn pale.

564–565 ***his whole . . . conceit:*** all of his activity creating outward appearances that express his thoughts.

571 ***cleave . . . speech:*** pierce everyone's ears with horrible words.

572 ***appall the free:*** terrify the innocent.

575 ***muddy-mettled:*** weak-spirited; ***peak:*** mope.

576 ***John-a-dreams:*** a dreamy idler; ***unpregnant of:*** not roused to action by.

579 ***defeat:*** destruction.

582–583 ***gives . . . lungs:*** calls me a complete liar.

could you not?

First Player. Ay, my lord.

Hamlet. Very well. Follow that lord—and look you mock
him not. [First Player *exits.*] My good friends, I'll leave
555   you till night. You are welcome to Elsinore.

Rosencrantz. Good my lord.

Hamlet. Ay, so, good-bye to you.

[Rosencrantz *and* Guildenstern *exit.*]

                               Now I am alone.
    O, what a rogue and peasant slave am I!
    Is it not monstrous that this player here,
560   But in a fiction, in a dream of passion,
    Could force his soul so to his own conceit
    That from her working all his visage wanned,
    Tears in his eyes, distraction in his aspect,
    A broken voice, and his whole function suiting
565   With forms to his conceit—and all for nothing!
    For Hecuba!
    What's Hecuba to him, or he to Hecuba,
    That he should weep for her? What would he do
    Had he the motive and the cue for passion
570   That I have? He would drown the stage with tears
    And cleave the general ear with horrid speech,
    Make mad the guilty and appall the free,
    Confound the ignorant and amaze indeed
    The very faculties of eyes and ears. Yet I,
575   A dull and muddy-mettled rascal, peak
    Like John-a-dreams, unpregnant of my cause,
    And can say nothing—no, not for a king
    Upon whose property and most dear life
    A damned defeat was made. Am I a coward?
580   Who calls me "villain"? breaks my pate across?
    Plucks off my beard and blows it in my face?
    Tweaks me by the nose? gives me the lie i' th' throat
    As deep as to the lungs? Who does me this?

584 **'Swounds:** by Christ's wounds (an oath).

585 **pigeon-livered:** meek as a pigeon.

587 **kites:** birds of prey.

588 **offal:** entrails.

589 **kindless:** unnatural.

591 **brave:** admirable. *What attitude do you think Hamlet is taking here?*

595 **drab:** prostitute.

596 **scullion:** kitchen servant.

597 **About:** get to work.

599 **cunning of the scene:** skill of the performance.

600 **presently:** immediately.

601 **malefactions:** crimes.

606 **tent . . . quick:** probe him in his most vulnerable spot; **blench:** flinch.

607–612 Hamlet wonders whether the devil, who has a very powerful effect on melancholy people, is deluding him to bring about his damnation.

612–613 **grounds . . . this:** a more solid basis for acting than the Ghost's words.

Ha! 'Swounds, I should take it! For it cannot be
585　But I am pigeon-livered and lack gall
To make oppression bitter, or ere this
I should have fatted all the region kites
With this slave's offal. Bloody, bawdy villain!
Remorseless, treacherous, lecherous, kindless villain!
590　O vengeance!
Why, what an ass am I! This is most brave,
That I, the son of a dear father murdered,
Prompted to my revenge by heaven and hell,
Must, like a whore, unpack my heart with words
595　And fall a-cursing like a very drab,
A scullion! Fie upon 't! Foh!
About, my brains!—Hum, I have heard
That guilty creatures sitting at a play
Have, by the very cunning of the scene,
600　Been struck so to the soul that presently
They have proclaimed their malefactions.
For murder, though it have no tongue, will speak
With most miraculous organ. I'll have these players
Play something like the murder of my father
605　Before mine uncle. I'll observe his looks;
I'll tent him to the quick. If he do blench,
I know my course. The spirit that I have seen
May be a devil, and the devil hath power
T' assume a pleasing shape; yea, and perhaps,
610　Out of my weakness and my melancholy,
As he is very potent with such spirits,
Abuses me to damn me. I'll have grounds
More relative than this. The play's the thing
Wherein I'll catch the conscience of the King.

[*He exits.*]

1 **drift of conference:** steering of conversation.

7 **forward to be sounded:** interested in being questioned.

ACT THREE

Scene 1 *The castle.*

Rosencrantz and Guildenstern report that they have failed to find the cause of Hamlet's strange behavior. Then, with Polonius and Claudius hiding nearby, Ophelia waits for Hamlet to arrive. Before noticing her, Hamlet meditates on death and uncertainty. He harshly rejects Ophelia, denouncing women and marriage. After he leaves, Claudius abandons the idea that Hamlet is in love. He tells Polonius that he plans to send Hamlet to England on a diplomatic mission. Polonius persuades him to wait until the Queen has had a chance to talk to Hamlet, with Polonius eavesdropping on their conversation.

[*Enter* King, Queen, Polonius, Ophelia, Rosencrantz, Guildenstern, *and* Lords.]

King. And can you by no drift of conference
  Get from him why he puts on this confusion,
  Grating so harshly all his days of quiet
  With turbulent and dangerous lunacy?

5 **Rosencrantz.** He does confess he feels himself distracted,
  But from what cause he will by no means speak.

Guildenstern. Nor do we find him forward to be sounded,
  But with a crafty madness keeps aloof
  When we would bring him on to some confession
10 Of his true state.

Queen.   Did he receive you well?

Rosencrantz. Most like a gentleman.

12 *forcing of his disposition:* effort.

13–14 *Niggard . . . reply:* Reluctant to talk, but willing to answer our questions.

15 *assay:* tempt.

17 *o'erraught:* overtook.

26 *give . . . edge:* sharpen his interest.

29 *closely:* privately.

31 *Affront:* meet.

32 *espials:* spies.

35 *as he is behaved:* according to his behavior.

Guildenstern. But with much forcing of his disposition.

Rosencrantz. Niggard of question, but of our demands
Most free in his reply.

15 **Queen.** Did you assay him to any pastime?

Rosencrantz. Madam, it so fell out that certain players
We o'erraught on the way. Of these we told him,
And there did seem in him a kind of joy
To hear of it. They are here about the court,
20 And, as I think, they have already order
This night to play before him.

Polonius.   'Tis most true,
And he beseeched me to entreat your Majesties
To hear and see the matter.

King. With all my heart, and it doth much content me
25 To hear him so inclined.
Good gentlemen, give him a further edge
And drive his purpose into these delights.

Rosencrantz. We shall, my lord.

[Rosencrantz *and* Guildenstern *and* Lords *exit.*]

King.   Sweet Gertrude, leave us too,
For we have closely sent for Hamlet hither,
30 That he, as 'twere by accident, may here
Affront Ophelia.
Her father and myself (lawful espials)
Will so bestow ourselves that, seeing unseen,
We may of their encounter frankly judge
35 And gather by him, as he is behaved,
If 't be th' affliction of his love or no
That thus he suffers for.

Queen.   I shall obey you.
And for your part, Ophelia, I do wish
That your good beauties be the happy cause
40 Of Hamlet's wildness. So shall I hope your virtues
Will bring him to his wonted way again,

43 *Gracious:* Your Grace (addressing the King).

44–49 Polonius tells Ophelia to read a religious book to provide an excuse for being alone. He remarks that many people are guilty of using worship and a devout appearance to cover their sins.

50–55 Claudius compares the heavy makeup that covers up the flaws on a prostitute's cheek to the beautiful words that cover his crime. *What does this speech reveal about his feelings?*

57 *To be:* To exist, to continue living.

59 *slings:* something thrown or shot.

64 *consummation:* final ending.

66 *rub:* obstacle.

68 *shuffled . . . coil:* cast aside the turmoil of life.

69–70 *There's . . . life:* That is the consideration that makes us endure misery (*calamity*) for such a long time.

To both your honors.

Ophelia.   Madam, I wish it may.

[Queen *exits.*]

Polonius. Ophelia, walk you here.—Gracious, so please
　　you,
　　We will bestow ourselves. [*To* Ophelia.] Read on this
　　book,
45　　That show of such an exercise may color
　　Your loneliness.—We are oft to blame in this
　　('Tis too much proved), that with devotion's visage
　　And pious action we do sugar o'er
　　The devil himself.

50　**King** [*aside*]. O, 'tis too true!
　　How smart a lash that speech doth give my conscience.
　　The harlot's cheek beautied with plast'ring art
　　Is not more ugly to the thing that helps it
　　Than is my deed to my most painted word.
55　　O heavy burden!

Polonius. I hear him coming. Let's withdraw, my lord.

[*They withdraw.*]

[*Enter* Hamlet.]

Hamlet. To be or not to be—that is the question:
　　Whether 'tis nobler in the mind to suffer
　　The slings and arrows of outrageous fortune,
60　　Or to take arms against a sea of troubles
　　And, by opposing, end them. To die, to sleep—
　　No more—and by a sleep to say we end
　　The heartache and the thousand natural shocks
　　That flesh is heir to—'tis a consummation
65　　Devoutly to be wished. To die, to sleep—
　　To sleep, perchance to dream. Ay, there's the rub,
　　For in that sleep of death what dreams may come,
　　When we have shuffled off this mortal coil,
　　Must give us pause. There's the respect

71 *time:* life in this world.

72 *contumely:* insults, expressions of contempt.

73 *despised:* unreturned.

74 *office:* officials.

74–75 *spurns . . . takes:* the insults that people of merit receive from the unworthy.

76–77 *When . . . bodkin:* when he might settle his accounts (*his quietus make*) with merely a dagger (*a bare bodkin*)—that is, end his unhappiness by killing himself.

77 *fardels:* burdens.

80 *bourn:* boundary.

81 *puzzles:* paralyzes.

85 *native hue:* natural color.

86 *cast:* shade.

87–89 *pitch and moment:* height and importance; *with this regard:* for this reason. *What do you think Hamlet has in mind when he speaks of great undertakings that have been diverted from their courses of action?*

89 *Soft you:* be quiet, enough.

90 *orisons:* prayers.

70   That makes calamity of so long life.
     For who would bear the whips and scorns of time,
     Th' oppressor's wrong, the proud man's contumely,
     The pangs of despised love, the law's delay,
     The insolence of office, and the spurns
75   That patient merit of th' unworthy takes,
     When he himself might his quietus make
     With a bare bodkin? Who would fardels bear,
     To grunt and sweat under a weary life,
     But that the dread of something after death,
80   The undiscovered country from whose bourn
     No traveler returns, puzzles the will
     And makes us rather bear those ills we have
     Than fly to others that we know not of?
     Thus conscience does make cowards of us all,
85   And thus the native hue of resolution
     Is sicklied o'er with the pale cast of thought,
     And enterprises of great pitch and moment
     With this regard their currents turn awry
     And lose the name of action.—Soft you now,
90   The fair Ophelia.—Nymph, in thy orisons
     Be all my sins remembered.

Ophelia.   Good my lord,
How does your Honor for this many a day?

Hamlet. I humbly thank you, well.

Ophelia. My lord, I have remembrances of yours
95   That I have longèd long to redeliver.
     I pray you now receive them.

Hamlet. No, not I. I never gave you aught.

Ophelia. My honored lord, you know right well you did,
     And with them words of so sweet breath composed
100 As made the things more rich. Their perfume lost,
     Take these again, for to the noble mind
     Rich gifts wax poor when givers prove unkind.
     There, my lord.

104 *honest:* truthful, chaste.

108 *Your honesty . . . beauty:* Your chastity should not allow itself to be influenced by your beauty.

109 *commerce:* dealings.

114 *his:* its.

115 *This . . . paradox:* This once went against the common viewpoint.

116 *time:* the present age.

118–120 Hamlet's metaphor is of grafting a branch onto a fruit tree: If virtue is grafted onto his sinful nature, the fruit of the grafted tree will still taste of his old nature.

122 *nunnery:* convent (sometimes used as a slang word for "brothel").

123 *indifferent honest:* reasonably virtuous.

127 *beck:* command.

Hamlet. Ha, ha, are you honest?

105 **Ophelia.** My lord?

Hamlet. Are you fair?

Ophelia. What means your lordship?

Hamlet. That if you be honest and fair, your honesty should admit no discourse to your beauty.

110 **Ophelia.** Could beauty, my lord, have better commerce than with honesty?

Hamlet. Ay, truly, for the power of beauty will sooner transform honesty from what it is to a bawd than the force of honesty can translate beauty into his
115 likeness. This was sometime a paradox, but now the time gives it proof. I did love you once.

Ophelia. Indeed, my lord, you made me believe so.

Hamlet. You should not have believed me, for virtue cannot so inoculate our old stock but we shall rel-
120 ish of it. I loved you not.

Ophelia. I was the more deceived.

Hamlet. Get thee to a nunnery. Why wouldst thou be a breeder of sinners? I am myself indifferent honest, but yet I could accuse me of such things that it
125 were better my mother had not borne me: I am very proud, revengeful, ambitious, with more offenses at my beck than I have thoughts to put them in, imagination to give them shape, or time to act them in. What should such fellows as I do
130 crawling between earth and heaven? We are arrant knaves all; believe none of us. Go thy ways to a nunnery. Where's your father?

Ophelia. At home, my lord.

Hamlet. Let the doors be shut upon him that he may
135 play the fool nowhere but in 's own house. Farewell.

139 *calumny:* slander, defamation.

142 *monsters:* horned cuckolds (men whose wives are unfaithful).

148 *nickname:* find new names for.

148–149 *make . . . ignorance:* use ignorance as an excuse for your waywardness.

155–158 Ophelia starts her description of Hamlet's former self by evoking the princely ideal of statesman, soldier, and scholar. He was the hope and ornament (***expectancy and rose***) of Denmark, a model of behavior and appearance for other people, respected (***observed***) by all who looked upon him.

163–164 *blown . . . ecstasy:* youth in full bloom withered by madness.

166 *affections:* feelings.

166–169 Claudius says that Hamlet's melancholy broods on something like a bird sits on an egg; he fears that some danger will hatch from it.

Ophelia. O, help him, you sweet heavens!

Hamlet. If thou dost marry, I'll give thee this plague
for thy dowry: be thou as chaste as ice, as pure as
snow, thou shalt not escape calumny. Get thee to a
140   nunnery, farewell. Or if thou wilt needs marry,
marry a fool, for wise men know well enough what
monsters you make of them. To a nunnery, go, and
quickly too. Farewell.

Ophelia. Heavenly powers, restore him!

145 **Hamlet.** I have heard of your paintings too, well
enough. God hath given you one face, and you
make yourselves another. You jig and amble, and
you lisp; you nickname God's creatures and make
your wantonness your ignorance. Go to, I'll no
150   more on 't. It hath made me mad. I say we will
have no more marriage. Those that are married
already, all but one, shall live. The rest shall keep
as they are. To a nunnery, go.

[*He exits.*]

Ophelia. O, what a noble mind is here o'erthrown!
155   The courtier's, soldier's, scholar's, eye, tongue, sword,
Th' expectancy and rose of the fair state,
The glass of fashion and the mold of form,
Th' observed of all observers, quite, quite down!
And I, of ladies most deject and wretched,
160   That sucked the honey of his musicked vows,
Now see that noble and most sovereign reason,
Like sweet bells jangled, out of time and harsh;
That unmatched form and stature of blown youth
Blasted with ecstasy. O, woe is me
165   T' have seen what I have seen, see what I see!

King [*advancing with* Polonius]. Love? His affections do
not that way tend;
Nor what he spake, though it lacked form a little,
Was not like madness. There's something in his soul

177 ***This . . . heart:*** this unknown thing that has settled in his heart.

187 ***be round:*** speak plainly.

189 ***find him not:*** does not learn what is disturbing him.

O'er which his melancholy sits on brood,
170 And I do doubt the hatch and the disclose
Will be some danger; which for to prevent,
I have in quick determination
Thus set it down: he shall with speed to England
For the demand of our neglected tribute.
175 Haply the seas, and countries different,
With variable objects, shall expel
This something-settled matter in his heart,
Whereon his brains still beating puts him thus
From fashion of himself. What think you on 't?

180 **Polonius.** It shall do well. But yet do I believe
The origin and commencement of his grief
Sprung from neglected love.—How now, Ophelia?
You need not tell us what Lord Hamlet said;
We heard it all.—My lord, do as you please,
185 But, if you hold it fit, after the play
Let his queen-mother all alone entreat him
To show his grief. Let her be round with him;
And I'll be placed, so please you, in the ear
Of all their conference. If she find him not,
190 To England send him, or confine him where
Your wisdom best shall think.

King.   It shall be so.
Madness in great ones must not unwatched go.

[*They exit.*]

3 *I had as lief:* I would just as soon.

9 *robustious:* boisterous.

9–10 *periwig-pated:* wig-wearing.

11 *groundlings:* the spectators who paid the cheapest price for admittance to the theater and stood in an open area in front of the stage.

14–15 *Termagant, Herod:* noisy, violent figures from early drama.

20 *modesty:* moderation.

21 *is from:* strays from.

Scene 2 *The castle.*

After instructing the actors on how to read their lines, Hamlet asks Horatio to observe Claudius during the performance. The court assembles, and the players act out silently a murder that greatly resembles Claudius's poisoning of King Hamlet. When they perform the same scene with dialogue, Claudius rises in distress and leaves. Hamlet is now convinced of his uncle's guilt. Rosencrantz and Guildenstern return to tell Hamlet that the King is angry and that the Queen wishes to speak with him in her chamber. Hamlet prepares to meet his mother, reminding himself that he must not harm her.

[*Enter* Hamlet *and three of the* Players.]

Hamlet. Speak the speech, I pray you, as I pronounced it to you, trippingly on the tongue; but if you mouth it, as many of our players do, I had as lief the town-crier spoke my lines. Nor do not saw the air too 5 much with your hand, thus, but use all gently; for in the very torrent, tempest, and, as I may say, whirl-wind of your passion, you must acquire and beget a temperance that may give it smoothness. O, it offends me to the soul to hear a robustious, periwig-10 pated fellow tear a passion to tatters, to very rags, to split the ears of the groundlings, who for the most part are capable of nothing but inexplicable dumb shows and noise. I would have such a fellow whipped for o'erdoing Termagant. It out-15 Herods Herod. Pray you, avoid it.

Player. I warrant your Honor.

Hamlet. Be not too tame neither, but let your own dis-cretion be your tutor. Suit the action to the word, the word to the action, with this special observance, 20 that you o'erstep not the modesty of nature. For anything so o'erdone is from the purpose of play-ing, whose end, both at the first and now, was and

Hamlet 133

24 *scorn:* something scornful.

25–26 *the very . . . pressure:* a true impression of the present.

26 *come tardy off:* done inadequately.

27 *the unskillful:* those lacking in judgment.

28–30 *the censure . . . others:* You should value the opinion of a single judicious theatergoer over an entire audience that lacks judgment.

30–37 Hamlet has seen performances by highly praised actors who so little resembled human beings onstage that he wonders whether they were created not by God but by some inferior workmen of nature.

38 *indifferently:* fairly well.

42 *of them:* some among them.

43 *barren:* dull-witted.

is to hold, as 'twere, the mirror up to nature, to show virtue her own feature, scorn her own image,

25 and the very age and body of the time his form and pressure. Now this overdone or come tardy off, though it makes the unskillful laugh, cannot but make the judicious grieve, the censure of the which one must in your allowance o'erweigh a whole theater

30 of others. O, there be players that I have seen play and heard others praise (and that highly), not to speak it profanely, that, neither having th' accent of Christians nor the gait of Christian, pagan, nor man, have so strutted and bellowed that I have

35 thought some of nature's journeymen had made men, and not made them well, they imitated humanity so abominably.

Player. I hope we have reformed that indifferently with us, sir.

40 **Hamlet.** O, reform it altogether. And let those that play your clowns speak no more than is set down for them, for there be of them that will themselves laugh, to set on some quantity of barren spectators to laugh too, though in the meantime some neces-

45 sary question of the play be then to be considered. That's villainous and shows a most pitiful ambition in the fool that uses it. Go make you ready.

[Players *exit.*]

[*Enter* Polonius, Guildenstern, *and* Rosencrantz.]

How now, my lord, will the King hear this piece of work?

50 **Polonius.** And the Queen too, and that presently.

Hamlet. Bid the players make haste. [Polonius *exits.*] Will you two help to hasten them?

Rosencrantz. Ay, my lord. They exit.

Hamlet. What ho, Horatio!

56–57 Hamlet says that Horatio is as honorable as any man he has ever dealt with.

62 *candied:* flattering.

63 *crook . . . knee:* bend the ready joint of the knee (kneel down).

64 *thrift:* profit.

68 *one . . . nothing:* one who experiences everything but is harmed by nothing.

71 *blood:* passions; *commeddled:* blended.

72 *pipe:* small wind instrument.

73 *stop:* a hole in a wind instrument that controls sound.

81 *Even . . . soul:* with your most searching observation.

82–86 Hamlet says that if Claudius's hidden (*occulted*) guilt does not reveal (*unkennel*) itself with the speech Hamlet wrote, then the Ghost is in league with the devil and Hamlet's thoughts about Claudius are as foul as the forge of the Roman god of metalworking.

[*Enter* Horatio.]

55 **Horatio.** Here, sweet lord, at your service.

Hamlet. Horatio, thou art e'en as just a man
As e'er my conversation coped withal.

Horatio. O, my dear lord—

Hamlet.   Nay, do not think I flatter,
For what advancement may I hope from thee
60 That no revenue hast but thy good spirits
To feed and clothe thee? Why should the poor be
    flattered?
No, let the candied tongue lick absurd pomp
And crook the pregnant hinges of the knee
Where thrift may follow fawning. Dost thou hear?
65 Since my dear soul was mistress of her choice
And could of men distinguish, her election
Hath sealed thee for herself. For thou hast been
As one in suffering all that suffers nothing,
A man that Fortune's buffets and rewards
70 Hast ta'en with equal thanks; and blessed are those
Whose blood and judgment are so well commeddled
That they are not a pipe for Fortune's finger
To sound what stop she please. Give me that man
That is not passion's slave, and I will wear him
75 In my heart's core, ay, in my heart of heart,
As I do thee.—Something too much of this.—
There is a play tonight before the King.
One scene of it comes near the circumstance
Which I have told thee of my father's death.
80 I prithee, when thou seest that act afoot,
Even with the very comment of thy soul
Observe my uncle. If his occulted guilt
Do not itself unkennel in one speech,
It is a damnèd ghost that we have seen,
85 And my imaginations are as foul
As Vulcan's stithy. Give him heedful note,
For I mine eyes will rivet to his face,

89 *censure of his seeming:* judgment of how he looks and behaves.

92 *be idle:* play the fool, be unoccupied.

94–97 Hamlet, taking *fares* to mean "feeds," answers that he eats promises. (Chameleons were said to feed on air.) *What promises do you think Hamlet is hinting at?*

98–99 Claudius complains that he can gain nothing from Hamlet's response.

108 *calf:* fool.

111 *metal more attractive:* a substance more magnetic.

And, after, we will both our judgments join
In censure of his seeming.

Horatio.   Well, my lord.
90   If he steal aught the whilst this play is playing
And 'scape detecting, I will pay the theft.

[*Sound a flourish.*]

Hamlet. They are coming to the play. I must be idle.
Get you a place.

[*Enter Trumpets and Kettle Drums. Enter* King, Queen,
Polonius, Ophelia, Rosencrantz, Guildenstern, *and other*
Lords *attendant with the* King's guard *carrying torches.*]

King. How fares our cousin Hamlet?

95   **Hamlet.** Excellent, i' faith, of the chameleon's dish. I
eat the air, promise-crammed. You cannot feed
capons so.

King. I have nothing with this answer, Hamlet. These
words are not mine.

100   **Hamlet.** No, nor mine now. [*To* Polonius.] My lord, you
played once i' th' university, you say?

Polonius. That did I, my lord, and was accounted a
good actor.

Hamlet. What did you enact?

105   **Polonius.** I did enact Julius Caesar. I was killed i' th'
Capitol. Brutus killed me.

Hamlet. It was a brute part of him to kill so capital a
calf there.—Be the players ready?

Rosencrantz. Ay, my lord. They stay upon your patience.

110   **Queen.** Come hither, my dear Hamlet, sit by me.

Hamlet. No, good mother. Here's metal more attractive.

[Hamlet *takes a place near* Ophelia.]

117 *country matters:* something coarse or indecent, which a rustic from the country might propose.

125 Hamlet sarcastically refers to himself as the best jig (comical song and dance) composer.

129–130 Hamlet ironically suggests giving up his mourning clothes for luxurious clothing trimmed with furs (*sables*—the dark color of which would in fact keep him dressed for mourning).

134 *not thinking on:* being forgotten; *hobby-horse:* a horse-and-rider figure who once performed in morris and may-day dances. Such traditions had been disappearing.

Dumb show: a scene without dialogue.

Polonius [*to the* King]. Oh, ho! Do you mark that?

Hamlet. Lady, shall I lie in your lap?

Ophelia. No, my lord.

115 **Hamlet.** I mean, my head upon your lap?

Ophelia. Ay, my lord.

Hamlet. Do you think I meant country matters?

Ophelia. I think nothing, my lord.

Hamlet. That's a fair thought to lie between maids' legs.

120 **Ophelia.** What is, my lord?

Hamlet. Nothing.

Ophelia. You are merry, my lord.

Hamlet. Who, I?

Ophelia. Ay, my lord.

125 **Hamlet.** O God, your only jig-maker. What should a man do but be merry? For look you how cheerfully my mother looks, and my father died within 's two hours.

Ophelia. Nay, 'tis twice two months, my lord.

Hamlet. So long? Nay, then, let the devil wear black, for
130 I'll have a suit of sables. O heavens, die two months ago, and not forgotten yet? Then there's hope a great man's memory may outlive his life half a year. But, by'r Lady, he must build churches, then, or else shall he suffer not thinking on, with the hobby-horse,whose
135 epitaph is "For oh, for oh, the hobby-horse is forgot."

[*The trumpets sound. Dumb show follows.*]

[*Enter a* King *and a* Queen, *very lovingly, the* Queen *embracing him and he her. She kneels and makes show of protestation unto him. He takes her up and declines his head upon her neck. He lies him down upon a bank of flowers. She, seeing him asleep, leaves him. Anon comes in another*

137 *miching mallecho:* sneaking misdeed. (The Spanish word *malhecho* means "misdeed.")

139 *Belike:* perhaps; *argument:* plot.

147 *naught:* naughty, indecent.

152 *posy of a ring:* a motto inscribed in a ring.

man, *takes off his crown, kisses it, pours poison in the sleeper's ears, and leaves him. The* Queen *returns, finds the* King *dead, makes passionate action. The* poisoner *with some three or four come in again, seem to condole with her. The dead body is carried away. The* poisoner *woos the* Queen *with gifts. She seems harsh awhile but in the end accepts his love.*]

[Players *exit.*]

Ophelia. What means this, my lord?

Hamlet. Marry, this is miching mallecho. It means mischief.

Ophelia. Belike this show imports the argument of the
140 play.

[*Enter* Prologue.]

Hamlet. We shall know by this fellow. The players cannot keep counsel; they'll tell all.

Ophelia. Will he tell us what this show meant?

Hamlet. Ay, or any show that you will show him. Be
145 not you ashamed to show, he'll not shame to tell you what it means.

Ophelia. You are naught, you are naught. I'll mark the play.

Prologue.

For us and for our tragedy,
150   Here stooping to your clemency,
We beg your hearing patiently.

[*He exits.*]

Hamlet. Is this a prologue or the posy of a ring?

Ophelia. 'Tis brief, my lord.

Hamlet. As woman's love.

155–160 The Player King says that they have been united in love and marriage for 30 years. ***Phoebus' cart:*** the sun god's chariot; ***Neptune's salt wash:*** the ocean; ***Tellus:*** Roman goddess of the earth; ***Hymen:*** god of marriage.

165 ***distrust you:*** am worried about you.

168–169 ***And women's . . . extremity:*** Women love and fear in equal measure, loving and fearing either too much or hardly at all.

175 ***My . . . do:*** My vital powers are no longer functioning.

176 ***behind:*** after I'm gone.

182 ***wormwood:*** a bitter herb.

183–184 ***The instances . . . love:*** People marry a second time for profit, not for love.

[*Enter the* Player King *and* Queen.]

155 **Player King.** *Full thirty times hath Phoebus' cart gone*
round
Neptune's salt wash and Tellus' orbèd ground,
And thirty dozen moons with borrowed sheen
About the world have times twelve thirties been
Since love our hearts and Hymen did our hands
160 *Unite commutual in most sacred bands.*

Player Queen. *So many journeys may the sun and*
moon
Make us again count o'er ere love be done!
But woe is me! You are so sick of late,
So far from cheer and from your former state,
165 *That I distrust you. Yet, though I distrust,*
Discomfort you, my lord, it nothing must.
For women fear too much, even as they love,
And women's fear and love hold quantity,
In neither aught, or in extremity.
170 *Now what my love is, proof hath made you*
know, And, as my love is sized, my fear is so:
Where love is great, the littlest doubts are fear;
Where little fears grow great, great love grows
there.

Player King. *Faith, I must leave thee, love, and shortly*
too.
175 *My operant powers their functions leave to do.*
And thou shalt live in this fair world behind,
Honored, beloved; and haply one as kind
For husband shalt thou—

Player Queen. O, *confound the rest!*
Such love must needs be treason in my breast.
180 *In second husband let me be accurst.*
None wed the second but who killed the first.

Hamlet. That's wormwood!

Player Queen. *The instances that second marriage move*

189–190 Our intentions are dependent on our memory; they are powerful at first (*Of violent birth*) but have little durability (*validity*).

193–194 *Most . . . debt:* We inevitably forget promises we have made to ourselves.

197–200 When the violence of extreme grief or joy ceases, so too does the willingness to act upon these emotions. People who feel extreme grief also feel extreme joy, and one passion is likely to follow another without much cause (*on slender accident*).

201 *for aye:* forever.

205 *The great . . . flies:* When a great man's fortune falls, his closest friend abandons him.

206 *advanced:* moving up in life.

207 *hitherto:* to this extent.

210 *Directly seasons him:* immediately changes him into.

213 *devices still:* plans always.

218 *Sport . . . night:* May the day deny (*lock from*) me its pastimes and night its rest.

Are base respects of thrift, but none of love.
185   *A second time I kill my husband dead*
    When second husband kisses me in bed.

Player King. *I do believe you think what now you speak,*
    But what we do determine oft we break.
    Purpose is but the slave to memory,
190   *Of violent birth, but poor validity,*
    Which now, the fruit unripe, sticks on the tree
    But fall unshaken when they mellow be.
    Most necessary 'tis that we forget
    To pay ourselves what to ourselves is debt.
195   *What to ourselves in passion we propose,*
    The passion ending, doth the purpose lose.
    The violence of either grief or joy
    Their own enactures with themselves destroy.
    Where joy most revels, grief doth most lament;
200   *Grief joys, joy grieves, on slender accident.*
    This world is not for aye, nor 'tis not strange
    That even our loves should with our fortunes change;
    For 'tis a question left us yet to prove
    Whether love lead fortune or else fortune love.
205   *The great man down, you mark his favorite flies;*
    The poor, advanced, makes friends of enemies.
    And hitherto doth love on fortune tend,
    For who not needs shall never lack a friend,
    And who in want a hollow friend doth try
210   *Directly seasons him his enemy.*
    But, orderly to end where I begun:
    Our wills and fates do so contrary run
    That our devices still are overthrown;
    Our thoughts are ours, their ends none of our own.
215   *So think thou wilt no second husband wed,*
    But die thy thoughts when thy first lord is dead.

Player Queen. *Nor earth to me give food, nor heaven*
      light,
    Sport and repose lock from me day and night,
    To desperation turn my trust and hope,

220 ***An anchor's cheer:*** a religious hermit's fare.

221–222 May each obstacle that turns the face of joy pale meet and destroy everything that I wish to see prosper (***what I would have well***).

231 ***doth protest too much:*** overstates her case, makes too many assurances.

233 ***argument:*** plot.

238 ***Tropically:*** metaphorically.

242 ***free:*** guilt-free.

243–244 ***Let . . . unwrung:*** a proverbial expression that means, "Let the guilty flinch; our consciences do not bother us."

220 *An anchor's cheer in prison be my scope.*
Each opposite that blanks the face of joy
Meet what I would have well and it destroy.
Both here and hence pursue me lasting strife,
If, once a widow, ever I be wife.

225 **Hamlet.** If she should break it now!

Player King. *'Tis deeply sworn. Sweet, leave me here*
   awhile.
My spirits grow dull, and fain I would beguile
The tedious day with sleep.

[*Sleeps.*]

Player Queen.   *Sleep rock thy brain,*
And never come mischance between us twain.

[*Player Queen exits.*]

230 **Hamlet.** Madam, how like you this play?

Queen. The lady doth protest too much, methinks.

Hamlet. O, but she'll keep her word.

King. Have you heard the argument? Is there no
offense in 't?

235 **Hamlet.** No, no, they do but jest, poison in jest. No
offense i' th' world.

King. What do you call the play?

Hamlet. "The Mousetrap." Marry, how? Tropically.
This play is the image of a murder done in Vienna.
240 Gonzago is the duke's name, his wife Baptista. You
shall see anon. 'Tis a knavish piece of work, but
what of that? Your Majesty and we that have free
souls, it touches us not. Let the galled jade wince;
our withers are unwrung.

[*Enter* Lucianus.]

245 This is one Lucianus, nephew to the king.

246 *chorus:* a character who explains what will happen in a play.

247–252 An "interpreter" is a narrator in a puppet show. Hamlet says that he could explain what is going on between Ophelia and her lover if he caught them together. When she comments that he is **keen** (sharp, penetrating), he responds with wordplay (using **keen** to mean "sexually aroused") that she finds even more witty but also more offensive. *Why do you think he is behaving this way?*

253 **mis-take:** take falsely. A reference to the marriage vow to take a husband "for better, for worse."

257 Time is my ally (**Confederate**) and only witness.

259 *Hecate's ban:* the curse of Hecate, goddess of witchcraft.

261 *usurp:* steal.

267 *false fire:* the discharge of a gun loaded without shot.

Ophelia. You are as good as a chorus, my lord.

Hamlet. I could interpret between you and your love, if I could see the puppets dallying.

Ophelia. You are keen, my lord, you are keen.

250 **Hamlet.** It would cost you a groaning to take off mine edge.

Ophelia. Still better and worse.

Hamlet. So you mis-take your husbands.—Begin, murderer. Pox, leave thy damnable faces and begin.
255 Come, the croaking raven doth bellow for revenge.

Lucianus. *Thoughts black, hands apt, drugs fit, and time agreeing,*
Confederate season, else no creature seeing,
Thou mixture rank, of midnight weeds collected,
With Hecate's ban thrice blasted, thrice infected,
260 *Thy natural magic and dire property*
On wholesome life usurp immediately.

[*Pours the poison in his ears.*]

Hamlet. He poisons him i' th' garden for his estate. His name's Gonzago. The story is extant and written in very choice Italian. You shall see anon how
265 the murderer gets the love of Gonzago's wife.

[Claudius *rises.*]

Ophelia. The King rises.

Hamlet. What, frighted with false fire?

Queen. How fares my lord?

Polonius. Give o'er the play.

270 **King.** Give me some light. Away!

Polonius. Lights, lights, lights!

[*All but* Hamlet *and* Horatio *exit.*]

273 ungallèd: uninjured.

277 turn Turk with me: turn against me. Elizabethan theater costumes often included feathers worn on hats and ribbon rosettes on shoes. A fellowship is a share or partnership in a theater company. (Shakespeare's shares in his company and in the Globe Theatre were his main sources of income.)

282 Damon: in Roman mythology the friend of Pythias.

285 pajock: either "peacock," which had a reputation for lust and cruelty, or "patchock," a savage person. (Presumably the rhyme Horatio hints at is **ass.**)

293 recorders: flute-like wooden wind instruments.

295 perdy: by God (from the French **par dieu**).

Hamlet. *Why, let the strucken deer go weep,*
    The hart ungallèd play.
  For some must watch, while some must sleep:
275   *Thus runs the world away.*
  Would not this, sir, and a forest of feathers (if the
  rest of my fortunes turn Turk with me) with two
  Provincial roses on my razed shoes, get me a fellowship in a cry of players?

280 **Horatio.** Half a share.

Hamlet. A whole one, I.
  For thou dost know, O Damon dear,
    This realm dismantled was
  Of Jove himself, and now reigns here
285   *A very very—pajock.*

Horatio. You might have rhymed.

Hamlet. O good Horatio, I'll take the ghost's word for
  a thousand pound. Didst perceive?

Horatio. Very well, my lord.

290 **Hamlet.** Upon the talk of the poisoning?

Horatio. I did very well note him.

Hamlet. Ah ha! Come, some music! Come, the
  recorders!
    For if the King like not the comedy,
295   *Why, then, belike he likes it not, perdy.*
  Come, some music!

[*Enter* Rosencrantz *and* Guildenstern.]

Guildenstern. Good my lord, vouchsafe me a word
  with you.

Hamlet. Sir, a whole history.

300 **Guildenstern.** The King, sir—

Hamlet. Ay, sir, what of him?

302 *distempered:* upset. (Hamlet takes it in the sense of "drunk.")

304 *choler:* anger. (Hamlet takes it in the sense of "biliousness.")

307 *purgation:* cleansing of the body of impurities; spiritual cleansing through confession.

310 *frame:* order; *start:* shy away like a nervous or wild horse.

318 *pardon:* permission to leave.

328 *admiration:* wonder.

332 *closet:* private room.

Guildenstern. Is in his retirement marvelous distempered.

Hamlet. With drink, sir?

Guildenstern. No, my lord, with choler.

305 **Hamlet.** Your wisdom should show itself more richer
to signify this to the doctor, for for me to put him
to his purgation would perhaps plunge him into
more choler.

Guildenstern. Good my lord, put your discourse into
310 some frame and start not so wildly from my affair.

Hamlet. I am tame, sir. Pronounce.

Guildenstern. The Queen your mother, in most great
affliction of spirit, hath sent me to you.

Hamlet. You are welcome.

315 **Guildenstern.** Nay, good my lord, this courtesy is not
of the right breed. If it shall please you to make me
a wholesome answer, I will do your mother's commandment. If not, your pardon and my return shall
be the end of my business.

320 **Hamlet.** Sir, I cannot.

Rosencrantz. What, my lord?

Hamlet. Make you a wholesome answer. My wit's dis-
eased. But, sir, such answer as I can make, you
shall command—or, rather, as you say, my mother.
325 Therefore no more but to the matter. My mother,
you say—

Rosencrantz. Then thus she says: your behavior hath
struck her into amazement and admiration.

Hamlet. O wonderful son that can so 'stonish a mother!
330 But is there no sequel at the heels of this mother's
admiration? Impart.

Rosencrantz. She desires to speak with you in her closet

337 *pickers and stealers:* hands (from the Church cate-
chism, "To keep my hands from picking and stealing").

345–346 The rest of the stale (*musty*) proverb is "the horse
starves," suggesting that Hamlet cannot wait so long.

348 *withdraw:* speak privately. Hamlet uses a hunting
metaphor: The hunter moves to the windward side of
the prey, causing it to flee toward a net (*toil*).

351–352 *if my . . . unmannerly:* If I'm behaving rudely, my bad
manners are due to my love for you.

360 *ventages:* stops, or finger holes, on the recorder.

ere you go to bed.

Hamlet. We shall obey, were she ten times our mother.
335   Have you any further trade with us?

Rosencrantz. My lord, you once did love me.

Hamlet. And do still, by these pickers and stealers.

Rosencrantz. Good my lord, what is your cause of distemper? You do surely bar the door upon your
340   own liberty if you deny your griefs to your friend.

Hamlet. Sir, I lack advancement.

Rosencrantz. How can that be, when you have the
voice of the King himself for your succession in
Denmark?

345 **Hamlet.** Ay, sir, but "While the grass grows"—the
proverb is something musty.

[*Enter the* Players *with recorders.*]

O, the recorders! Let me see one. [*He takes a
recorder and turns to* Guildenstern.] To withdraw
with you: why do you go about to recover the
350   wind of me, as if you would drive me into a toil?

Guildenstern. O, my lord, if my duty be too bold, my
love is too unmannerly.

Hamlet. I do not well understand that. Will you play
upon this pipe?

355 **Guildenstern.** My lord, I cannot.

Hamlet. I pray you.

Guildenstern. Believe me, I cannot.

Hamlet. I do beseech you.

Guildenstern. I know no touch of it, my lord.

360 **Hamlet.** It is as easy as lying. Govern these ventages
with your fingers and thumb, give it breath with

369–375 ***sound me:*** play upon me like an instrument, investigate me; ***compass:*** an instrument's range; ***organ:*** musical instrument; ***fret me:*** annoy me (also punning on ***frets,*** the raised bars for fingering a stringed instrument). *What point is Hamlet making with this musical metaphor?*

387 ***fool . . . bent:*** make me play the fool to the limits of my ability.

388 ***by and by:*** before long.

your mouth, and it will discourse most eloquent
music. Look you, these are the stops.

Guildenstern. But these cannot I command to any
utt'rance of harmony. I have not the skill.

Hamlet. Why, look you now, how unworthy a thing
you make of me! You would play upon me, you
would seem to know my stops, you would pluck
out the heart of my mystery, you would sound me
from my lowest note to the top of my compass;
and there is much music, excellent voice, in this little organ, yet cannot you make it speak. 'Sblood,
do you think I am easier to be played on than a
pipe? Call me what instrument you will, though
you can fret me, you cannot play upon me.

[*Enter* Polonius.]

God bless you, sir.

Polonius. My lord, the Queen would speak with you,
and presently.

Hamlet. Do you see yonder cloud that's almost in
shape of a camel?

Polonius. By th' Mass, and 'tis like a camel indeed.

Hamlet. Methinks it is like a weasel.

Polonius. It is backed like a weasel.

Hamlet. Or like a whale.

Polonius. Very like a whale.

Hamlet. Then I will come to my mother by and by.
[*Aside.*] They fool me to the top of my bent.—I will
come by and by.

Polonius. I will say so.

Hamlet. "By and by" is easily said. Leave me, friends.

[*All but* Hamlet *exit.*]

397 ***Nero:*** a Roman emperor who put his mother to death.

401–402 Hamlet tells himself that however much she is rebuked (***shent***) in his words, he must not put those words into action (***give them seals***).

1 ***him:*** his behavior.

3 ***forthwith dispatch:*** have prepared at once.

'Tis now the very witching time of night,
When churchyards yawn and hell itself breathes out
Contagion to this world. Now could I drink hot
    blood
And do such bitter business as the day
395   Would quake to look on. Soft, now to my mother.
O heart, lose not thy nature; let not ever
The soul of Nero enter this firm bosom.
Let me be cruel, not unnatural.
I will speak daggers to her, but use none.
400   My tongue and soul in this be hypocrites:
How in my words somever she be shent,
To give them seals never, my soul, consent.

[*He exits.*]

Scene 3 *The castle.*

*Claudius tells Rosencrantz and Guildenstern that they will
soon be taking Hamlet to England. Polonius informs
Claudius that he is going to the Queen's chamber, where
he will eavesdrop on her conversation with Hamlet.
Alone, Claudius wonders whether he could obtain
spiritual forgiveness for murdering his brother if he
continues to profit from that crime. As he kneels down to
pray, Hamlet enters the room and takes out his sword.
Thinking, however, that Claudius might go to heaven if
he is killed while at prayer, Hamlet decides to put off his
vengeance until he catches his uncle during a sinful
moment, which would surely damn him. After Hamlet
leaves, Claudius reveals that he is unable to pray.*

[*Enter* King, Rosencrantz, *and* Guildenstern.]

King. I like him not, nor stands it safe with us
    To let his madness range. Therefore prepare you.
    I your commission will forthwith dispatch,
    And he to England shall along with you.

5 ***The terms of our estate:*** my position as king.

6 ***near 's:*** near us.

11 ***single and particular:*** individual and private.

13 ***noyance:*** harm.

14 ***weal:*** well-being.

15 ***cess:*** cessation, decease.

16 ***gulf:*** whirlpool.

17–22 Rosencrantz alludes to Fortune's massive (***massy***) wheel, with the king traditionally shown on the top; when the king falls, everyone connected with him plunges as well.

24 ***Arm you:*** prepare yourelf.

29 ***process:*** proceedings; ***tax him home:*** strongly rebuke him.

31 ***meet:*** fitting.

33 ***of vantage:*** in addition.

The terms of our estate may not endure
Hazard so near 's as doth hourly grow
Out of his brows.

Guildenstern.   We will ourselves provide.
Most holy and religious fear it is
To keep those many many bodies safe
10   That live and feed upon your Majesty.

Rosencrantz. The single and peculiar life is bound
With all the strength and armor of the mind
To keep itself from noyance, but much more
That spirit upon whose weal depends and rests
15   The lives of many. The cess of majesty
Dies not alone, but like a gulf doth draw
What's near it with it; or it is a massy wheel
Fixed on the summit of the highest mount,
To whose huge spokes ten thousand lesser things
20   Are mortised and adjoined, which, when it falls,
Each small annexment, petty consequence,
Attends the boist'rous ruin. Never alone
Did the king sigh, but with a general groan.

King. Arm you, I pray you, to this speedy voyage,
25   For we will fetters put about this fear,
Which now goes too free-footed.

Rosencrantz.   We will haste us.

[Rosencrantz *and* Guildenstern *exit.*]

[*Enter* Polonius.]

Polonius. My lord, he's going to his mother's closet.
Behind the arras I'll convey myself
To hear the process. I'll warrant she'll tax him home;
30   And, as you said (and wisely was it said),
'Tis meet that some more audience than a mother,
Since nature makes them partial, should o'erhear
The speech of vantage. Fare you well, my liege.
I'll call upon you ere you go to bed
35   And tell you what I know.

37 *primal eldest curse:* the curse of Cain (the son of Adam and Eve who murdered his brother Abel).

46–47 *Whereto . . . offense:* What purpose does mercy serve other than to oppose condemnation?

48–50 Claudius says that the two functions of prayer are to prevent us from sinning and to gain forgiveness once we have fallen.

56 *th' offense:* the benefits of the crime.

57–64 In the corrupt ways (*currents*) of this world, the offender's gold-bearing hand can push aside justice, and often the law is bought out by the wealth gained through wickedness. But that isn't the case in heaven (*above*), where there is no evasion (*shuffling*); the true nature of every deed lies exposed, and we are forced to testify against ourselves without concealing any faults.

64 *rests:* remains.

68 *limèd:* trapped like a bird caught in quicklime (a sticky substance smeared on branches).

69 *engaged:* entangled; *Make assay:* Make an attempt (addressed to himself).

King.   Thanks, dear my lord.

[Polonius *exits.*]

O, my offense is rank, it smells to heaven;
It hath the primal eldest curse upon 't,
A brother's murder. Pray can I not,
Though inclination be as sharp as will.
40   My stronger guilt defeats my strong intent,
And, like a man to double business bound,
I stand in pause where I shall first begin
And both neglect. What if this cursèd hand
Were thicker than itself with brother's blood?
45   Is there not rain enough in the sweet heavens
To wash it white as snow? Whereto serves mercy
But to confront the visage of offense?
And what's in prayer but this twofold force,
To be forestallèd ere we come to fall,
50   Or pardoned being down? Then I'll look up.
My fault is past. But, O, what form of prayer
Can serve my turn? "Forgive me my foul murder"?
That cannot be, since I am still possessed
Of those effects for which I did the murder:
55   My crown, mine own ambition, and my queen.
May one be pardoned and retain th' offense?
In the corrupted currents of this world,
Offense's gilded hand may shove by justice,
And oft 'tis seen the wicked prize itself
60   Buys out the law. But 'tis not so above:
There is no shuffling; there the action lies
In his true nature, and we ourselves compelled,
Even to the teeth and forehead of our faults,
To give in evidence. What then? What rests?
65   Try what repentance can. What can it not?
Yet what can it, when one cannot repent?
O wretched state! O bosom black as death!
O limèd soul, that, struggling to be free,
Art more engaged! Help, angels! Make assay.
70   Bow, stubborn knees, and heart with strings of steel

73 *pat:* conveniently.

75 *would be scanned:* needs to be looked at carefully.

79 *hire and salary:* something Claudius should pay me to do.

80–84 Hamlet complains that his father was killed without allowing him spiritual preparation (***grossly***). He was immersed in worldly pleasures (***full of bread***) and his sins were in full bloom (***broad blown***). Only heaven knows how his final account (***audit***) stands, but from Hamlet's perspective his father's sins seem a heavy burden. *What does Hamlet fear for his father?*

86 *seasoned:* prepared.

88 *know thou a more horrid hent:* wait to be grasped on a more horrible occasion.

95 *stays:* awaits me.

96 *physic:* medicine (referring to the postponement of revenge or to Claudius's act of prayer).

Be soft as sinews of the newborn babe.
All may be well.

[*He kneels.*]

[*Enter* Hamlet.]

Hamlet. Now might I do it pat, now he is a-praying,
And now I'll do 't.

[*He draws his sword.*]

                 And so he goes to heaven,
75   And so am I revenged. That would be scanned:
A villain kills my father, and for that,
I, his sole son, do this same villain send
To heaven.
Why, this is hire and salary, not revenge.
80   He took my father grossly, full of bread,
With all his crimes broad blown, as flush as May;
And how his audit stands who knows save heaven.
But in our circumstance and course of thought
'Tis heavy with him. And am I then revenged
85   To take him in the purging of his soul,
When he is fit and seasoned for his passage?
No.
Up sword, and know thou a more horrid hent.

[*He sheathes his sword.*]

When he is drunk asleep, or in his rage,
90   Or in th' incestuous pleasure of his bed,
At game a-swearing, or about some act
That has no relish of salvation in 't—
Then trip him, that his heels may kick at heaven,
And that his soul may be as damned and black
95   As hell, whereto it goes. My mother stays.
This physic but prolongs thy sickly days.

[Hamlet *exits.*]

King [*rising*]. My words fly up, my thoughts remain
    below;

1 **straight:** right away; **lay home to:** strongly rebuke.

2 **broad:** unrestrained.

5 **round:** blunt.

Words without thoughts never to heaven go.

[*He exits.*]

Scene 4 *The Queen's private chamber.*

Polonius hides behind a tapestry in Queen Gertrude's room. Hamlet arrives and greets his mother with harsh language, alarming her and causing Polonius to cry out for help. Hamlet thrusts his sword through the tapestry. He is disappointed when he finds out that he has murdered Polonius rather than Claudius. Hamlet condemns his mother for marrying Claudius, comparing the latter's vices to the virtues of her late husband. As the Queen begs him to stop, the Ghost appears and urges Hamlet to carry out his vengeance. Gertrude, who cannot see or hear anything, assumes her son is hallucinating. After the Ghost leaves, Hamlet asks his mother to repent her sins and stay away from Claudius's bed. He tells her his suspicions about his upcoming journey to England, then drags Polonius's body from the room.

[*Enter* Queen *and* Polonius.]

Polonius. He will come straight. Look you lay home
    to him.
    Tell him his pranks have been too broad to bear with
    And that your Grace hath screened and stood
      between
    Much heat and him. I'll silence me even here.
5   Pray you, be round with him.

Hamlet [*within*]. Mother, mother, mother!

Queen. I'll warrant you. Fear me not. Withdraw,
    I hear him coming.

[Polonius *hides behind the arras.*]

[*Enter* Hamlet.]

12 *idle:* foolish.

15 *forgot me:* forgotten who I am; *rood:* cross.

20 *glass:* mirror.

25 *Dead for a ducat:* I'll wager a ducat that I kill him; I'll kill him for a ducat.

31 *Why do you think the Queen repeats these words when Hamlet accuses her of killing the king?*

Hamlet. Now, mother, what's the matter?

10 **Queen.** Hamlet, thou hast thy father much offended.

Hamlet. Mother, you have my father much offended.

Queen. Come, come, you answer with an idle tongue.

Hamlet. Go, go, you question with a wicked tongue.

Queen. Why, how now, Hamlet?

Hamlet.   What's the matter now?

15 **Queen.** Have you forgot me?

Hamlet.   No, by the rood, not so.
You are the Queen, your husband's brother's wife,
And (would it were not so) you are my mother.

Queen. Nay, then I'll set those to you that can speak.

Hamlet. Come, come, and sit you down; you shall not
    budge.
20 You go not till I set you up a glass
    Where you may see the inmost part of you.

Queen. What wilt thou do? Thou wilt not murder me?
    Help, ho!

Polonius. [*behind the arras*]. What ho! Help!

25 **Hamlet.** How now, a rat? Dead for a ducat, dead.

[*He kills* Polonius *by thrusting a rapier through the arras.*]

Polonius. [*behind the arras*]. O, I am slain!

Queen.   O me, what hast thou done?

Hamlet. Nay, I know not. Is it the King?

Queen. O, what a rash and bloody deed is this!

Hamlet. A bloody deed—almost as bad, good mother,
30 As kill a king and marry with his brother.

Queen. As kill a king?

34 *too busy:* too much of a busybody.

38–39 *If . . . sense:* if habitual wickedness (***damnèd custom***) has not so hardened (***brazed***) your heart that it has become armor (***proof***) and fortification against feeling (***sense***).

47 *contraction:* the marriage contract.

48 *sweet religion:* marriage vows.

49 *rhapsody:* senseless jumble.

49–52 Heaven's face looks down shamefully (***with heated visage***) at the world (***this solidity and compound mass***) as if it were doomsday, and is sick with sorrow from thinking of the deed (remarriage of Gertrude).

53 *index:* introduction.

55 *counterfeit presentment:* portraits.

57 *Hyperion:* the sun god; ***front:*** brow.

59–60 *A station . . . hill:* a stance like that of the winged messenger of the gods.

172   **Literature Connections**

Hamlet.   Ay, lady, it was my word.

[*He pulls* Polonius' *body from behind the arras.*]

Thou wretched, rash, intruding fool, farewell.
I took thee for thy better. Take thy fortune.
Thou find'st to be too busy is some danger.

[*To* Queen.]

35   Leave wringing of your hands. Peace, sit you down,
And let me wring your heart; for so I shall
If it be made of penetrable stuff,
If damnèd custom have not brazed it so
That it be proof and bulwark against sense.

40   **Queen.** What have I done, that thou dar'st wag thy
tongue
In noise so rude against me?

Hamlet.   Such an act
That blurs the grace and blush of modesty,
Calls virtue hypocrite, takes off the rose
From the fair forehead of an innocent love
45   And sets a blister there, makes marriage vows
As false as dicers' oaths—O, such a deed
As from the body of contraction plucks
The very soul, and sweet religion makes
A rhapsody of words! Heaven's face does glow
50   O'er this solidity and compound mass
With heated visage, as against the doom,
Is thought-sick at the act.

Queen.   Ay me, what act
That roars so loud and thunders in the index?

Hamlet. Look here upon this picture and on this,
55   The counterfeit presentment of two brothers.
See what a grace was seated on this brow,
Hyperion's curls, the front of Jove himself,
An eye like Mars' to threaten and command,
A station like the herald Mercury

65–66 Hamlet uses the metaphor of a mildewed **ear** of grain that is blighting (***blasting***) a nearby healthy plant.

68 ***batten on:*** grow fat from feeding on; ***moor:*** barren land.

70 ***heyday in the blood:*** sexual excitement.

72–78 Hamlet says that her senses must be paralyzed (***apoplexed***), because madness or hallucination (***sense to ecstasy***) would still leave her enough judgment to make the right choice between Claudius and Hamlet's father. He wonders what devil tricked (***cozened***) her in a game of blindman's bluff (presumably by steering her toward Claudius).

80 ***sans all:*** without the other senses.

82 ***so mope:*** be so dazed.

83–89 If hell can stir up rebellion (***mutine***) in an older woman's bones, then in young people virtue should be like a candle melting in its own flame. There is no shame when youth acts impetuously, since the frost of old age burns just as hot, and reason, instead of restraining desire (***will***), urges it on.

92 ***grainèd:*** ingrained, indelible.

93 ***leave their tinct:*** lose their color, fade.

94 ***enseamèd:*** greasy, sweaty.

60   New-lighted on a heaven-kissing hill,
      A combination and a form indeed
      Where every god did seem to set his seal
      To give the world assurance of a man.
      This was your husband. Look you now what follows.
65   Here is your husband, like a mildewed ear
      Blasting his wholesome brother. Have you eyes?
      Could you on this fair mountain leave to feed
      And batten on this moor? Ha! Have you eyes?
      You cannot call it love, for at your age
70   The heyday in the blood is tame, it's humble
      And waits upon the judgment; and what judgment
      Would step from this to this? Sense sure you have,
      Else could you not have motion; but sure that sense
      Is apoplexed; for madness would not err,
75   Nor sense to ecstasy was ne'er so thralled,
      But it reserved some quantity of choice
      To serve in such a difference. What devil was 't
      That thus hath cozened you at hoodman-blind?
      Eyes without feeling, feeling without sight,
80   Ears without hands or eyes, smelling sans all,
      Or but a sickly part of one true sense
      Could not so mope. O shame, where is thy blush?
      Rebellious hell,
      If thou canst mutine in a matron's bones,
85   To flaming youth let virtue be as wax
      And melt in her own fire. Proclaim no shame
      When the compulsive ardor gives the charge,
      Since frost itself as actively doth burn,
      And reason panders will.

90   **Queen.** O Hamlet, speak no more!
      Thou turn'st my eyes into my very soul,
      And there I see such black and grainèd spots
      As will not leave their tinct.

      Hamlet.   Nay, but to live
      In the rank sweat of an enseamèd bed,
95   Stewed in corruption, honeying and making love

100 *tithe:* tenth part.

101 *vice:* buffoon. (The Vice was a clownish villain in medieval morality plays.)

102 *cutpurse:* thief.

103 *diadem:* crown.

106 *shreds and patches:* referring to the patchwork costume of clowns or fools.

111 *lapsed in time and passion:* having let time pass and my passion cool.

116 *amazement:* bewilderment, shock.

118 *Conceit:* imagination.

122 *incorporal:* immaterial.

124–126 Like solders awakened by an alarm, your smoothly laid (*bedded*) hair—as if there were life in this outgrowth (*excrements*)—jumps up and stands on end.

Over the nasty sty!

Queen. O, speak to me no more!
These words like daggers enter in my ears.
No more, sweet Hamlet!

Hamlet. A murderer and a villain,
100   A slave that is not twentieth part the tithe
Of your precedent lord; a vice of kings,
A cutpurse of the empire and the rule,
That from a shelf the precious diadem stole
And put it in his pocket—

105 **Queen.** No more!

Hamlet. A king of shreds and patches—

[*Enter* Ghost.]

Save me and hover o'er me with your wings,
You heavenly guards!—What would your gracious
  figure?

Queen. Alas, he's mad.

110 **Hamlet.** Do you not come your tardy son to chide,
That, lapsed in time and passion, lets go by
Th' important acting of your dread command?
O, say!

Ghost. Do not forget. This visitation
115   Is but to whet thy almost blunted purpose.
But look, amazement on thy mother sits.
O, step between her and her fighting soul.
Conceit in weakest bodies strongest works.
Speak to her, Hamlet.

Hamlet. How is it with you, lady?

120 **Queen.** Alas, how is 't with you,
That you do bend your eye on vacancy
And with th' incorporal air do hold discourse?
Forth at your eyes your spirits wildly peep,
And, as the sleeping soldiers in th' alarm,

130 conjoined: joined together.

131 them capable: the stones responsive.

132–133 convert . . . effects: alter the stern impression I give.

134 want: lack.

141 in his habit as he lived: in the clothes he wore when alive.

144–145 Madness (*ecstasy*) is very skillful at creating this kind of hallucination (*bodiless creation*).

148–155 Hamlet tells his mother to make him repeat his description word for word, a test that madness would skip (*gambol*) away from. He asks her not to use his madness rather than her misdeeds to explain this visitation; such a soothing ointment (*unction*) would merely cover up the sore on her soul, allowing the infection within to grow unseen.

125 Your bedded hair, like life in excrements,
Start up and stand an end. O gentle son,
Upon the heat and flame of thy distemper
Sprinkle cool patience! Whereon do you look?

Hamlet. On him, on him! Look you how pale he glares.
130 His form and cause conjoined, preaching to stones,
Would make them capable. [*To the Ghost*]. Do not
look upon me,
Lest with this piteous action you convert
My stern effects. Then what I have to do
Will want true color—tears perchance for blood.

135 **Queen.** To whom do you speak this?

Hamlet. Do you see nothing there?

Queen. Nothing at all; yet all that is I see.

Hamlet. Nor did you nothing hear?

Queen. No, nothing but ourselves.

140 **Hamlet.** Why, look you there, look how it steals away!
My father, in his habit as he lived!
Look where he goes even now out at the portal!

[Ghost *exits.*]

Queen. This is the very coinage of your brain.
This bodiless creation ecstasy
145 Is very cunning in.

Hamlet.   Ecstasy?
My pulse as yours doth temperately keep time
And makes as healthful music. It is not madness
That I have uttered. Bring me to the test,
And I the matter will reword, which madness
150 Would gambol from. Mother, for love of grace,
Lay not that flattering unction to your soul
That not your trespass but my madness speaks.
It will but skin and film the ulcerous place,
Whiles rank corruption, mining all within,

158 *this my virtue:* my virtuous talk.

159 *fatness:* grossness; *pursy:* flabby, bloated.

161 *curb:* bow; *leave:* permission.

167–171 Custom, which consumes our awareness of the evil we habitually do, can also make us grow used to performing good actions.

174 *stamp of nature:* the traits we are born with.

175 A word seems to be missing in this line. Some editors have suggested inserting *master, curb,* or *lodge* after *either.*

180 *this:* Polonius.

181 *their scourge and minister:* heaven's agent of retribution.

182 *answer well:* explain.

185 *remains behind:* is still to come.

187–194 Hamlet lists the things he wants Gertrude to avoid doing.

155 Infects unseen. Confess yourself to heaven,
Repent what's past, avoid what is to come,
And do not spread the compost on the weeds
To make them ranker. Forgive me this my virtue,
For, in the fatness of these pursy times,
160 Virtue itself of vice must pardon beg,
Yea, curb and woo for leave to do him good.

Queen. O Hamlet, thou hast cleft my heart in twain!

Hamlet. O, throw away the worser part of it,
And live the purer with the other half!
165 Good night. But go not to my uncle's bed.
Assume a virtue if you have it not.
That monster, custom, who all sense doth eat,
Of habits devil, is angel yet in this,
That to the use of actions fair and good
170 He likewise gives a frock or livery
That aptly is put on. Refrain tonight,
And that shall lend a kind of easiness
To the next abstinence, the next more easy;
For use almost can change the stamp of nature
175 And either . . . the devil or throw him out
With wondrous potency. Once more, good night,
And, when you are desirous to be blest,
I'll blessing beg of you. For this same lord

[*Pointing to* Polonius.]

I do repent; but heaven hath pleased it so
180 To punish me with this and this with me,
That I must be their scourge and minister.
I will bestow him and will answer well
The death I gave him. So, again, good night.
I must be cruel only to be kind.
185 This bad begins, and worse remains behind.
One word more, good lady.

Queen.   What shall I do?

Hamlet. Not this by no means that I bid you do:

188 *bloat:* bloated.

189 *mouse:* a term of endearment.

190 *reechy:* filthy.

191 *paddling in:* fingering on.

194 *in craft:* by clever design or action.

194–202 Although Hamlet has asked his mother not to let Claudius use sexual attentions to unravel the secret that Hamlet is only pretending to be mad, he now sarcastically urges her to go ahead and tell Claudius, wondering why she should hide such important matters from a toad (*paddock*), a bat, or a tomcat (*gib*). He refers to a story about an ape that died trying to imitate the flight of birds it released from a cage, hinting that the Queen will get hurt if she lets out her secret.

208–211 Rosencrantz and Guildenstern have been commanded to escort (*sweep my way*) and conduct (*marshall*) Hamlet to some treachery planned against him.

212–213 *to have . . . petard:* to have the maker of military devices blown up (*hoist*) by his own bomb (*petard*).

213–214 *and 't . . . I will:* unless I have bad luck I will; *mines:* tunnels.

216 *crafts:* plots, crafty schemes.

217 Polonius's death will force Hamlet to leave in a hurry.

Let the bloat king tempt you again to bed,
Pinch wanton on your cheek, call you his mouse,
190 And let him, for a pair of reechy kisses
Or paddling in your neck with his damned fingers,
Make you to ravel all this matter out
That I essentially am not in madness,
But mad in craft. 'Twere good you let him know,
195 For who that's but a queen, fair, sober, wise,
Would from a paddock, from a bat, a gib,
Such dear concernings hide? Who would do so?
No, in despite of sense and secrecy,
Unpeg the basket on the house's top,
200 Let the birds fly, and like the famous ape,
To try conclusions, in the basket creep
And break your own neck down.

Queen. Be thou assured, if words be made of breath
And breath of life, I have no life to breathe
205 What thou hast said to me.

Hamlet. I must to England, you know that.

Queen.   Alack,
I had forgot! 'Tis so concluded on.

Hamlet. There's letters sealed; and my two schoolfel-
lows,
Whom I will trust as I will adders fanged,
210 They bear the mandate; they must sweep my way
And marshal me to knavery. Let it work,
For 'tis the sport to have the enginer
Hoist with his own petard; and 't shall go hard
But I will delve one yard below their mines
215 And blow them at the moon. O, 'tis most sweet
When in one line two crafts directly meet.
This man shall set me packing.
I'll lug the guts into the neighbor room.
Mother, good night indeed. This counselor
220 Is now most still, most secret, and most grave,
Who was in life a foolish prating knave.—

222 *to draw toward an end :* to finish up.

Come, sir, to draw toward an end with you.
Good night, mother.

[*They exit,* Hamlet *tugging in* Polonius.]

1 *matter:* significance.

11 *brainish apprehension:* frenzied belief.

17–19 Claudius worries that the death will be blamed on him (*laid to us*) because he should have had the foresight (*providence*) to keep Hamlet restrained (*short*) and isolated (*out of haunt*).

ACT FOUR

Scene 1 *The Castle.*

Gertrude tells Claudius that Hamlet has killed Polonius. He sends Rosencrantz and Guildenstern to recover the body.

[*Enter* King *and* Queen, *with* Rosencrantz *and* Guildenstern.]

King. There's matter in these sighs; these profound
    heaves
  You must translate; 'tis fit we understand them.
  Where is your son?

Queen. Bestow this place on us a little while.

[Rosencrantz *and* Guildenstern *exit.*]

5   Ah, mine own lord, what have I seen tonight!

King. What, Gertrude? How does Hamlet?

Queen. Mad as the sea and wind when both contend
  Which is the mightier. In his lawless fit,
  Behind the arras hearing something stir,
10 Whips out his rapier, cries "A rat, a rat,"
  And in this brainish apprehension kills
  The unseen good old man.

King.   O heavy deed!
  It had been so with us, had we been there.
  His liberty is full of threats to all—
15 To you yourself, to us, to everyone.
  Alas, how shall this bloody deed be answered?
  It will be laid to us, whose providence

22 *divulging:* being revealed.

25–26 *ore . . . mineral:* vein of gold in a mine.

32 *countenance:* accept.

33 *some further aid:* others who can help.

40–44 Some words are missing after "untimely done" in line 41. Many editors insert "So haply slander" or a similar phrase. Claudius is hoping that slander, which hits as directly as a cannon fired at point-blank range hits its target, will miss the royal household.

Should have kept short, restrained, and out of haunt
This mad young man. But so much was our love,
20 We would not understand what was most fit,
But, like the owner of a foul disease,
To keep it from divulging, let it feed
Even on the pith of life. Where is he gone?

Queen. To draw apart the body he hath killed,
25 O'er whom his very madness, like some ore
Among a mineral of metals base,
Shows itself pure: he weeps for what is done.

King. O Gertrude, come away!
The sun no sooner shall the mountains touch
30 But we will ship him hence; and this vile deed
We must with all our majesty and skill
Both countenance and excuse.—Ho, Guildenstern!

[*Enter* Rosencrantz *and* Guildenstern.]

Friends both, go join you with some further aid.
Hamlet in madness hath Polonius slain,
35 And from his mother's closet hath he dragged him.
Go seek him out, speak fair, and bring the body
Into the chapel. I pray you, haste in this.

[Rosencrantz *and* Guildenstern *exit.*]

Come, Gertrude, we'll call up our wisest friends
And let them know both what we mean to do
40 And what's untimely done. . . .
Whose whisper o'er the world's diameter,
As level as the cannon to his blank
Transports his poisoned shot, may miss our name
And hit the woundless air. O, come away!
45 My soul is full of discord and dismay.

[*They exit.*]

6 *compounded:* mixed. Hamlet alludes to Genesis 3.19: "dust thou art, and unto dust shalt thou return."

12 *demanded of:* questioned by.

13 *replication:* response.

15 *countenance:* favor.

17–18 *like an ape . . . jaw:* as an ape keeps food in the corner of its mouth.

Scene 2 *The Castle.*

Hamlet, refusing to tell Rosencrantz and Guildenstern where the body is, offers to go with them to the King.

[*Enter* Hamlet.]

Hamlet. Safely stowed.

Gentlemen [*within*] Hamlet! Lord Hamlet!

Hamlet. But soft, what noise? Who calls on Hamlet?
O, here they come.

[*Enter* Rosencrantz, Guildenstern, *and others.*]

5 **Rosencrantz.** What have you done, my lord, with the
    dead body?

Hamlet. Compounded it with dust, whereto 'tis kin.

Rosencrantz. Tell us where 'tis, that we may take it
    thence
And bear it to the chapel.

Hamlet. Do not believe it.

10 **Rosencrantz.** Believe what?

Hamlet. That I can keep your counsel and not mine
    own. Besides, to be demanded of a sponge, what
    replication should be made by the son of a king?

Rosencrantz. Take you me for a sponge, my lord?

15 **Hamlet.** Ay, sir, that soaks up the King's countenance,
    his rewards, his authorities. But such officers do
    the King best service in the end. He keeps them like
    an ape an apple in the corner of his jaw, first
    mouthed, to be last swallowed. When he needs
20   what you have gleaned, it is but squeezing you,
    and, sponge, you shall be dry again.

Rosencrantz. I understand you not, my lord.

23 *sleeps in:* is meaningless to.

27–28 Hamlet may be playing off the idea that the king occupies two "bodies": his own mortal body and the office of kingship. Claudius is a king of no account (*of nothing*); the office of kingship does not belong to him.

30 *Hide fox . . . after:* a cry from a children's game such as hide-and-seek.

4–5 *He's loved . . . eyes:* He's loved by the confused masses, who choose not by judgment but by appearance.

6 *scourge:* punishment.

7 *To bear . . . even:* to manage everything smoothly and evenly.

9 *Deliberate pause:* carefully thought out.

9–11 *Diseases . . . all:* Desperate diseases require desperate remedies.

Hamlet. I am glad of it. A knavish speech sleeps in a
foolish ear.

25 **Rosencrantz.** My lord, you must tell us where the
body is and go with us to the King.

Hamlet. The body is with the King, but the King is
not with the body. The King is a thing—

Guildenstern. A "thing," my lord?

30 **Hamlet.** Of nothing. Bring me to him. Hide fox, and
all after!

[*They exit.*]

Scene 3 *The castle.*

*Hamlet finally reveals where he has hidden Polonius's
body. Claudius tells him that he must depart immediately
for England. Left alone, Claudius contemplates his plot to
have the English kill Hamlet when he arrives.*

[*Enter* King *and two or three.*]

King. I have sent to seek him and to find the body.
How dangerous is it that this man goes loose!
Yet must not we put the strong law on him.
He's loved of the distracted multitude,
5   Who like not in their judgment, but their eyes;
And, where 'tis so, th' offender's scourge is weighed,
But never the offense. To bear all smooth and even,
This sudden sending him away must seem
Deliberate pause. Diseases desperate grown
10   By desperate appliance are relieved
Or not at all.

[*Enter* Rosencrantz.]

How now, what hath befallen?

Rosencrantz. Where the dead body is bestowed, my lord,

19–21 Hamlet says that a group of crafty (*politic*) worms are dining on him.

21 *Your . . . diet:* Worms have the last word when it comes to eating.

24 *but variable service:* only different courses (of a meal).

32 *progress:* royal journey.

We cannot get from him.

King. But where is he?

Rosencrantz. Without, my lord; guarded, to know
your pleasure.

15 **King.** Bring him before us.

Rosencrantz. Ho! Bring in the lord.

[*They enter with* Hamlet.]

King. Now, Hamlet, where's Polonius?

Hamlet. At supper.

King. At supper where?

Hamlet. Not where he eats, but where he is eaten. A
20 certain convocation of politic worms are e'en at
him. Your worm is your only emperor for diet. We
fat all creatures else to fat us, and we fat ourselves
for maggots. Your fat king and your lean beggar is
but variable service—two dishes but to one table.
25 That's the end.

King. Alas, alas!

Hamlet. A man may fish with the worm that hath eat
of a king and eat of the fish that hath fed of that
worm.

30 **King.** What dost thou mean by this?

Hamlet. Nothing but to show you how a king may go
a progress through the guts of a beggar.

King. Where is Polonius?

Hamlet. In heaven. Send thither to see. If your messen-
35 ger find him not there, seek him i' th' other place
yourself. But if, indeed, you find him not within
this month, you shall nose him as you go up the
stairs into the lobby.

42 ***tender:*** regard, hold dear.

45–47 Claudius says that the sailing vessel (***bark***) is ready, the wind is favorable (***at help***), his fellow travellers wait (***tend***) for him, and everything is ready (***bent***).

52 ***cherub:*** angel of knowledge. *What do you think Hamlet is hinting with this response?*

57 ***at foot:*** closely.

60 ***leans on:*** is related to.

61–68 Claudius says that if the King of England values Claudius's love (which Denmark's great power should make the English King value, since the military defeat, or scar [***cicatrice***], Denmark gave England is still unhealed and England voluntarily pays tribute [***homage***] to Denmark), he—the King of England—will not regard with indifference (***coldly set***) Claudius's command to have Hamlet killed immediately.

King [*to* Attendants]. Go, seek him there.

40 **Hamlet.** He will stay till you come.

[Attendants *exit.*]

King. Hamlet, this deed, for thine especial safety
(Which we do tender, as we dearly grieve
For that which thou hast done) must send thee hence
With fiery quickness. Therefore prepare thyself.
45 The bark is ready, and the wind at help,
Th' associates tend, and everything is bent
For England.

Hamlet. For England?

King. Ay, Hamlet.

50 **Hamlet.** Good.

King. So is it, if thou knew'st our purposes.

Hamlet. I see a cherub that sees them. But come, for
England.
Farewell, dear mother.

King.   Thy loving father, Hamlet.

Hamlet. My mother. Father and mother is man and wife,
55 Man and wife is one flesh, and so, my mother.—
Come, for England.

[*He exits.*]

King. Follow him at foot; tempt him with speed aboard.
Delay it not. I'll have him hence tonight.
Away, for everything is sealed and done
60 That else leans on th' affair. Pray you, make haste.

[*All but the* King *exit.*]

And England, if my love thou hold'st at aught
(As my great power thereof may give thee sense,
Since yet thy cicatrice looks raw and red
After the Danish sword, and thy free awe

69 *hectic:* fever.

71 *Howe'er my haps:* whatever my fortunes.

2 *license:* permission.

3 *the conveyance of:* escort during.

5–7 Fortinbras says that if the King wishes to see him, he will show his respect in person (*in his eye*).

9 *softly:* slowly, carefully.

10 *powers:* forces.

65 Pays homage to us), thou mayst not coldly set
Our sovereign process, which imports at full,
By letters congruing to that effect,
The present death of Hamlet. Do it, England,
For like the hectic in my blood he rages,
70 And thou must cure me. Till I know 'tis done,
Howe'er my haps, my joys were ne'er begun.

[*He exits.*]

Scene 4 *Near the coast of Denmark.*

On the way to his ship, Hamlet encounters Prince Fortinbras's army, which is marching toward Poland to battle over a worthless piece of land. Comparing his own inaction with Fortinbras's eagerness to fight for honor, Hamlet vows that henceforth he will only think bloody thoughts.

[*Enter* Fortinbras *with his army over the stage.*]

Fortinbras. Go, Captain, from me greet the Danish king.
Tell him that by his license Fortinbras
Craves the conveyance of a promised march
Over his kingdom. You know the rendezvous.
5 If that his Majesty would aught with us,
We shall express our duty in his eye;
And let him know so.

Captain. I will do 't, my lord.

Fortinbras. Go softly on.

[*All but the* Captain *exit.*]

[*Enter* Hamlet, Rosencrantz, Guildenstern, *and others.*]

10 **Hamlet.** Good sir, whose powers are these?

Captain. They are of Norway, sir.

16 *the main:* the main part.

18 *Truly . . . addition:* to speak plainly.

21 *To pay . . . it:* I would not pay even five ducats a year to rent it.

23 *ranker:* higher; *in fee:* outright.

27 *Will not . . . straw:* are not enough to settle this trifling dispute.

28 *impostume:* puss-filled swelling.

29 *without:* on the outside.

34 *inform against:* denounce.

36 *market:* profit.

38–41 *Sure He . . . unused:* God would not have given us such a considerable power of reasoning to let it grow moldy from lack of use.

Hamlet. How purposed, sir, I pray you?

Captain. Against some part of Poland.

Hamlet. Who commands them, sir?

15 **Captain.** The nephew to old Norway, Fortinbras.

Hamlet. Goes it against the main of Poland, sir,
Or for some frontier?

Captain. Truly to speak, and with no addition,
We go to gain a little patch of ground
20 That hath in it no profit but the name.
To pay five ducats, five, I would not farm it;
Nor will it yield to Norway or the Pole
A ranker rate, should it be sold in fee.

Hamlet. Why, then, the Polack never will defend it.

25 **Captain.** Yes, it is already garrisoned.

Hamlet. Two thousand souls and twenty thousand ducats
Will not debate the question of this straw.
This is th' impostume of much wealth and peace,
That inward breaks and shows no cause without
30 Why the man dies.—I humbly thank you, sir.

Captain. God be wi' you, sir.

[*He exits.*]

Rosencrantz. Will 't please you go, my lord?

Hamlet. I'll be with you straight. Go a little before.

[*All but* Hamlet *exit.*]

How all occasions do inform against me
35 And spur my dull revenge. What is a man
If his chief good and market of his time
Be but to sleep and feed? A beast, no more.
Sure He that made us with such large discourse,
Looking before and after, gave us not
40 That capability and godlike reason

42–43 *Bestial . . . event:* beast-like forgetfulness or cowardly hesitation from thinking too carefully about the outcome.

48 *gross:* obvious.

52 *Makes mouths . . . event:* makes scornful faces at the unforeseeable outcome.

55–58 True greatness does not lie in refraining from action when there is no great cause but in the willingness to fight whenever honor is at stake.

63 *fantasy and trick of fame:* illusion of honor.

65–67 *Whereon . . . slain:* The disputed land does not have enough room for so many men to battle on and is too small a burial ground to hold those who will be killed.

To fust in us unused. Now whether it be
Bestial oblivion or some craven scruple
Of thinking too precisely on th' event
(A thought which, quartered, hath but one part
   wisdom
45   And ever three parts coward), I do not know
Why yet I live to say "This thing's to do,"
Sith I have cause, and will, and strength, and means
To do 't. Examples gross as earth exhort me:
Witness this army of such mass and charge,
50   Led by a delicate and tender prince,
Whose spirit with divine amibition puffed
Makes mouths at the invisible event,
Exposing what is mortal and unsure
To all that fortune, death, and danger dare,
55   Even for an eggshell. Rightly to be great
Is not to stir without great argument,
But greatly to find quarrel in a straw
When honor's at the stake. How stand I, then,
That have a father killed, a mother stained,
60   Excitements of my reason and my blood,
And let all sleep, while to my shame I see
The imminent death of twenty thousand men
That for a fantasy and trick of fame
Go to their graves like beds, fight for a plot
65   Whereon the numbers cannot try the cause,
Which is not tomb enough and continent
To hide the slain? O, from this time forth
My thoughts be bloody or be nothing worth!

[*He exits.*]

3 *distract:* distracted; *mood . . . pitied:* state of mind must be pitied.

6 *tricks:* deception.

7 *Spurns enviously at straws:* takes offense at trifles; *in doubt:* without clear meaning.

8–14 Although Ophelia speaks nonsense, her confused manner of speaking moves her listeners to gather some meaning by patching her words together to fit their conjectures. Her words, together with her gestures and expressions, might arouse suspicions that would be unfortunate even if unproven.

16 *ill-breeding:* intent on making trouble.

Scene 5 *The castle.*

Gertrude, told that Ophelia has gone mad, agrees to see her. Ophelia sings about a lost lover and sexual betrayal. After she exits, Claudius describes the scandal resulting from the hasty burial of Polonius. Laertes breaks into the room and demands to find out what happened to his father. Claudius has begun to calm him down when Ophelia returns, still behaving madly. She leaves again, and Claudius insists that he is innocent of Polonius's death.

[*Enter* Horatio, Queen, *and a* Gentleman.]

Queen. I will not speak with her.

Gentleman. She is importunate,
    Indeed distract; her mood will needs be pitied.

Queen. What would she have?

5 **Gentleman.** She speaks much of her father, says she hears
    There's tricks i' th' world, and hems, and beats her
        heart,
    Spurns enviously at straws, speaks things in doubt
    That carry but half sense. Her speech is nothing,
    Yet the unshaped use of it doth move
10   The hearers to collection. They aim at it
    And botch the words up fit to their own thoughts;
    Which, as her winks and nods and gestures yield them,
    Indeed would make one think there might be thought,
    Though nothing sure, yet much unhappily.

15 **Horatio.** 'Twere good she were spoken with, for she
        may strew
    Dangerous conjectures in ill-breeding minds.

Queen. Let her come in.

[Gentleman *exits.*]

    [*Aside*] To my sick soul (as sin's true nature is),

19 *toy:* trifle; *amiss:* misfortune.

20–21 Guilt is so full of clumsy suspicion (*artless jealousy*) that it reveals (*spills*) itself through fear of being revealed.

26 *cockle hat:* a hat with a scallop shell (worn by pilgrims to show that they had been to an overseas shrine).

27 *shoon:* shoes.

28 *imports:* means.

39 *Larded:* decorated.

41 *showers:* tears.

43 *God dild you:* God yield, or reward, you.

43–44 Ophelia refers to a legend about a baker's daughter who was turned into an owl because she refused to give Christ bread.

46 *Conceit:* brooding.

Each toy seems prologue to some great amiss.
20   So full of artless jealousy is guilt,
It spills itself in fearing to be spilt.

[*Enter* Ophelia *distracted.*]

Ophelia. Where is the beauteous Majesty of Denmark?

Queen. How now, Ophelia?

Ophelia [*sings*]. *How should I your true love know*
25   *From another one?*
                  By his cockle hat and staff
                  And his sandal shoon.

Queen. Alas, sweet lady, what imports this song?

Ophelia. Say you? Nay, pray you, mark.
30   [*Sings.*] *He is dead and gone, lady,*
                  He is dead and gone;
                  At his head a grass-green turf,
                  At his heels a stone.
Oh, ho!

35 **Queen.** Nay, but Ophelia—

Ophelia. Pray you, mark.

       [*Sings.*] *White his shroud as the mountain snow—*

[*Enter* King.]

Queen. Alas, look here, my lord.

Ophelia. [*sings*] *Larded all with sweet flowers;*
40   *Which bewept to the ground did not go*
                  With true-love showers.

King. How do you, pretty lady?

Ophelia. Well, God dild you. They say the owl was a
baker's daughter. Lord, we know what we are but
45   know not what we may be. God be at your table.

King. Conceit upon her father.

49–67 This song refers to the ancient custom that the first maiden a man sees on St. Valentine's Day will be his sweetheart.

50 *betime:* early.

54 *dupped:* opened.

59 *Gis:* Jesus.

62 *Cock:* a substitution for "God" in oaths.

63 *tumbled:* had sexual intercourse with.

67 *An:* if.

Ophelia. Pray let's have no words of this, but when
they ask you what it means, say you this:
[*Sings.*] *Tomorrow is Saint Valentine's day,*
50   *All in the morning betime,*
And I a maid at your window,
         To be your Valentine.
Then up he rose and donned his clothes
         And dupped the chamber door,
55 *Let in the maid, that out a maid*
         Never departed more.

King. Pretty Ophelia—

Ophelia. Indeed, without an oath, I'll make an end on 't:
[*Sings.*] *By Gis and by Saint Charity,*
60   *Alack and fie for shame,*
Young men will do 't, if they come to 't;
         By Cock, they are to blame.
Quoth she "Before you tumbled me,
         You promised me to wed."
65 He answers:
"So would I 'a done, by yonder sun,
         An thou hadst not come to my bed."

King. How long hath she been thus?

Ophelia. I hope all will be well. We must be patient,
70 but I cannot choose but weep to think they would
lay him i' th' cold ground. My brother shall know
of it. And so I thank you for your good counsel.
Come, my coach! Good night, ladies, good night,
sweet ladies, good night, good night.

[*She exits.*]

75 **King.** Follow her close; give her good watch, I pray you.

[Horatio *exits.*]

O, this is the poison of deep grief. It springs
All from her father's death, and now behold!
O Gertrude, Gertrude,

79 *spies:* soldiers sent ahead as scouts.

82 *muddied:* confused.

84–85 Claudius says that he has only acted foolishly (**greenly**) by burying Polonius in haste and secrecy (**hugger-mugger**).

89–95 Laertes, who has secretly returned from France, is clouded by suspicion and does not lack gossipers (**buzzers**) who spread rumors of his father's death. And in the absence of facts (**of matter beggared**), the need for some explanation means that there will be no hesitation in publicly accusing me (**our person**) of the crime.

96 *murd'ring piece:* a cannon that can kill many men simultaneously with its scattered shot.

97 *Gives . . . death:* kills me over and over.

100 *Switzers:* Swiss bodyguards.

102–105 Laertes is overpowering Claudius's officers as quickly as the ocean, rising above its boundary (**list**), floods the level ground.

106–108 *as the world . . . word:* as if the world had just begun, and ancient tradition and custom, which should confirm and support everything one says, were both forgotten.

When sorrows come, they come not single spies,
80 But in battalions: first, her father slain;
Next, your son gone, and he most violent author
Of his own just remove; the people muddied,
Thick, and unwholesome in their thoughts and
    whispers
For good Polonius' death, and we have done but
    greenly
85 In hugger-mugger to inter him; poor Ophelia
Divided from herself and her fair judgment,
Without the which we are pictures or mere beasts;
Last, and as much containing as all these,
Her brother is in secret come from France,
90 Feeds on his wonder, keeps himself in clouds,
And wants not buzzers to infect his ear
With pestilent speeches of his father's death,
Wherein necessity, of matter beggared,
Will nothing stick our person to arraign
95 In ear and ear. O, my dear Gertrude, this,
Like to a murd'ring piece, in many places
Gives me superfluous death.

[*A noise within.*]

Queen. Alack, what noise is this?

King. Attend!
100 Where is my Switzers? Let them guard the door.

[*Enter a* Messenger.]

What is the matter?

Messenger.   Save yourself, my lord.
The ocean, overpeering of his list,
Eats not the flats with more impiteous haste
Than young Laertes, in a riotous head,
105 O'erbears your officers. The rabble call him "lord,"
And, as the world were now but to begin,
Antiquity forgot, custom not known,
The ratifiers and props of every word,

110 *Caps:* caps thrown into the air.

113 *counter:* a hunting term that means "to follow a trail in the wrong direction."

121–124 Laertes reacts in extreme terms to the Queen's urging him to calm down, saying that no true son could be calm about his father's murder—that being calm would in effect prove that son to be a bastard.

122 *cuckold:* a man whose wife is unfaithful.

124 *true:* faithful.

126–129 Claudius tells Gertrude not to fear for his personal safety; so much divinity protects (***doth hedge***) a king that treason can only peer (***peep***) from afar at what it would like to do. *Do you think this speech reflects Claudius's true feelings?*

They cry "Choose we, Laertes shall be king!"
110　Caps, hands, and tongues applaud it to the clouds,
　　"Laertes shall be king! Laertes king!"

[*A noise within.*]

Queen. How cheerfully on the false trail they cry.
　　O, this is counter, you false Danish dogs!

King. The doors are broke.

[*Enter* Laertes *with others.*]

115　**Laertes.** Where is this king?—Sirs, stand you all without.

All. No, let's come in!

Laertes. I pray you, give me leave.

All. We will, we will.

Laertes. I thank you. Keep the door. [Followers *exit.*] O,
　　thou vile king,
120　Give me my father!

Queen.　　　　　　　Calmly, good Laertes.

Laertes. That drop of blood that's calm proclaims me
　　bastard,
　　Cries "cuckold" to my father, brands the harlot
　　Even here between the chaste unsmirchèd brow
　　Of my true mother.

King.　　　　　　　What is the cause, Laertes,
125　That thy rebellion looks so giant-like?—
　　Let him go, Gertrude. Do not fear our person.
　　There's such divinity doth hedge a king
　　That treason can but peep to what it would,
　　Acts little of his will.—Tell me, Laertes,
130　Why thou art thus incensed.—Let him go,
　　　Gertrude.—
　　Speak, man.

Laertes. Where is my father?

135 *juggled with:* played with, deceived.

138–141 Laertes says he does not care what happens to him in this world or the next; he only wants thorough revenge.

144 *husband:* manage, conserve.

148 *swoopstake:* a gambling term that means taking all the stakes on the gambling table.

153 *pelican:* traditionally thought to feed its young with its own blood.

157 *sensibly:* feelingly.
158 *level:* plain.

King. Dead.

Queen. But not by him.

King.   Let him demand his fill.

135 **Laertes.** How came he dead? I'll not be juggled with.
   To hell, allegiance! Vows, to the blackest devil!
   Conscience and grace, to the profoundest pit!
   I dare damnation. To this point I stand,
   That both the worlds I give to negligence,
140 Let come what comes, only I'll be revenged
   Most throughly for my father.

King. Who shall stay you?

Laertes. My will, not all the world.
   And for my means, I'll husband them so well
145 They shall go far with little.

King.   Good Laertes,
   If you desire to know the certainty
   Of your dear father, is 't writ in your revenge
   That, swoopstake, you will draw both friend and
      foe,
   Winner and loser?

150 **Laertes.** None but his enemies.

King. Will you know them, then?

Laertes. To his good friends thus wide I'll ope my arms
   And, like the kind life-rend'ring pelican,
   Repast them with my blood.

King.   Why, now you speak
155 Like a good child and a true gentleman.
   That I am guiltless of your father's death
   And am most sensibly in grief for it,
   It shall as level to your judgment 'pear
   As day does to your eye.

                    [*A noise within*] Let her come in.

162 *virtue:* power.

163–164 In his vow to revenge Ophelia's madness, Laertes uses the image of weights being placed on a scale to make it tilt in the opposite direction.

168–169 *fine in:* refined by; *instance:* token (suggesting that Ophelia has sent her sanity into the grave with her father).

175 *persuade:* argue rationally for.

176 *move thus:* have such an effect.

177–178 Ophelia assigns refrains to the others so they can join in the singing.

178 *the wheel:* perhaps referring to the refrain or a spinning wheel that accompanies the singing.

181 *This . . . matter:* This nonsense has more meaning than rational speech.

182–192 Ophelia distributes flowers among the other characters. Each flower would have had symbolic meaning for an Elizabethan audience. *Rosemary* was used to symbolize remembrance at funerals. *Pansies,* a name derived from the French word for thought, *pensée,* was associated with courtship. Ophelia also mentions *fennel* (flattery), *columbines* (adultery or ingratitude), *rue* (repentance, sorrow), the *daisy* (dissembling, false love) and *violets* (faithfulness).

185–186 Laertes finds a lesson (*document*) in Ophelia's linking of thoughts and remembrance.

190 *with a difference:* a variation in a coat of arms to distinguish among different branches in a family. (Ophelia may be suggesting that the person to whom she gives the rue has a different cause for sorrow or repentance.)

160 **Laertes.** How now, what noise is that?

[*Enter* Ophelia.]

O heat, dry up my brains! Tears seven times salt
Burn out the sense and virtue of mine eye!
By heaven, thy madness shall be paid with weight
Till our scale turn the beam! O rose of May,
165 Dear maid, kind sister, sweet Ophelia!
O heavens, is 't possible a young maid's wits
Should be as mortal as an old man's life?
Nature is fine in love, and, where 'tis fine,
It sends some precious instance of itself
170 After the thing it loves.

Ophelia [*sings*]. *They bore him barefaced on the bier,*
Hey non nonny, nonny, hey nonny,
And in his grave rained many a tear.
Fare you well, my dove.

175 **Laertes.** Hadst thou thy wits and didst persuade revenge,
It could not move thus.

Ophelia. You must sing "A-down a-down"—and you
"Call him a-down-a."—O, how the wheel becomes
it! It is the false steward that stole his master's
180 daughter.

Laertes. This nothing's more than matter.

Ophelia. There's rosemary, that's for remembrance.
Pray you, love, remember. And there is pansies,
that's for thoughts.

185 **Laertes.** A document in madness: thoughts and
remembrance fitted.

Ophelia. There's fennel for you, and columbines.
There's rue for you, and here's some for me; we
may call it herb of grace o' Sundays. You must
190 wear your rue with a difference. There's a daisy. I
would give you some violets, but they withered all
when my father died. They say he made a good end.

194 *Thought:* melancholy; ***passion:*** suffering.

202 ***flaxen:*** pale yellow; ***poll:*** head.

204 ***cast away:*** scatter uselessly.

213 ***collateral:*** indirect.

214 ***find us touched:*** find me implicated.

221–222 The traditional burial ceremony (***ostentation***) for a
knight included hanging his helmet, sword, and a tablet
displaying his coat of arms (***hatchment***) over the tomb.

[*Sings.*] *For bonny sweet Robin is all my joy.*

Laertes. Thought and afflictions, passion, hell itself
195   She turns to favor and to prettiness.

Ophelia [*sings*].
     And will he not come again?
     And will he not come again?
       No, no, he is dead.
       Go to thy deathbed.
200 *He never will come again.*

     His beard was as white as snow,
     All flaxen was his poll.
       He is gone, he is gone,
       And we cast away moan.
205 *God 'a mercy on his soul.*
     And of all Christians' souls, I pray God. God be
     wi' you.

[*She exits.*]

Laertes. Do you see this, O God?

King. Laertes, I must commune with your grief,
210   Or you deny me right. Go but apart,
       Make choice of whom your wisest friends you will,
       And they shall hear and judge 'twixt you and me.
       If by direct or by collateral hand
       They find us touched, we will our kingdom give,
215   Our crown, our life, and all that we call ours,
       To you in satisfaction; but if not,
       Be you content to lend your patience to us,
       And we shall jointly labor with your soul
       To give it due content.

Laertes.   Let this be so.
220   His means of death, his obscure funeral
       (No trophy, sword, nor hatchment o'er his bones,
       No noble rite nor formal ostentation)
       Cry to be heard, as 'twere from heaven to earth,

224 ***That I . . . question:*** so that I must demand an explanation.

9 ***an't:*** if it.

10 ***th' ambassador:*** Hamlet.

14 ***overlooked:*** read; ***means:*** means of access.

16–17 ***pirate . . . appointment:*** pirate ship well equipped for warfare.

That I must call 't in question.

King.   So you shall,
225   And where th' offense is, let the great ax fall.
       I pray you, go with me.

[*They exit.*]

Scene 6 *The castle.*

*Some sailors bring Horatio a letter from Hamlet, who
writes that he is being held in Denmark by pirates.
Horatio takes the sailors to see the King.*

[*Enter* Horatio *and others.*]

Horatio. What are they that would speak with me?

Gentleman. Seafaring men, sir. They say they have letters for you.

Horatio. Let them come in. [Gentleman *exits.*] I do not
5   know from what part of the world I should be
     greeted, if not from Lord Hamlet.

[*Enter* Sailors.]

Sailor. God bless you, sir.

Horatio. Let Him bless thee too.

Sailor. He shall, sir, an 't please Him. There's a letter
10   for you, sir. It came from th' ambassador that was
      bound for England—if your name be Horatio, as I
      am let to know it is.

[*He hands* Horatio *a letter.*]

Horatio [*reads the letter*]. *Horatio, when thou shalt
have overlooked this, give these fellows some means
15   to the King. They have letters for him. Ere we
      were two days old at sea, a pirate of very warlike
      appointment gave us chase. Finding ourselves too*

21 *thieves of mercy:* merciful thieves.

22 *they knew what they did:* their actions were calculated.

24 *repair:* come.

27 *light . . . bore:* inadequate for the importance.

32 *way:* means of access.

1 *my acquittance seal:* confirm my innocence.

3 *Sith:* since.

slow of sail, we put on a compelled valor, and in the
grapple I boarded them. On the instant, they got
20 *clear of our ship; so I alone became their prisoner.*
They have dealt with me like thieves of mercy, but
they knew what they did: I am to do a good turn
for them. Let the King have the letters I have sent,
and repair thou to me with as much speed as thou
25 *wouldst fly death. I have words to speak in thine*
ear will make thee dumb; yet are they much too
light for the bore of the matter. These good fellows
will bring thee where I am. Rosencrantz and
Guildenstern hold their course for England; of
30 *them I have much to tell thee. Farewell.*
He that thou knowest thine, Hamlet.

Come, I will give you way for these your letters
And do 't the speedier that you may direct me
To him from whom you brought them.

[*They exit.*]

Scene 7 *The castle.*

Claudius tells Laertes that he has refrained from taking
action because of Hamlet's popularity and the Queen's
love for him. A messenger arrives with letters from
Hamlet explaining that he is back in Denmark. Claudius
proposes that Laertes challenge Hamlet to a fencing
match, with Laertes secretly using a sharp and poisoned
sword. Claudius will back Laertes up by giving Hamlet
poisoned wine. The Queen enters and tells them that
Ophelia has drowned.

[*Enter* King *and* Laertes.]

King. Now must your conscience my acquittance seal,
And you must put me in your heart for friend,
Sith you have heard, and with a knowing ear,
That he which hath your noble father slain

7 *capital:* punishable by death.

8 *safety:* concern for your safety.

9 *mainly:* greatly.

11 *unsinewed:* weak.

15 *conjunctive:* closely joined.

16 *star . . . sphere:* According to Ptolemaic astronomy, which was still widely believed in Shakespeare's time, each planet moves around the Earth in a hollow sphere.

18 *count:* account, indictment.

19–25 Claudius says that the common people (***general gender***), through their love for Hamlet, act like a spring with such a high concentration of lime that wood placed in it will become petrified; they change his limitations (***gyves***) into attractive qualities, so that the strong wind of their approval would blow back any arrows that Claudius might shoot at Hamlet.

27 *terms:* condition.

28–30 *Whose worth . . . perfections:* If praises can recall Ophelia's former self, her worth placed her at the top of the age.

5 Pursued my life.

Laertes.   It well appears. But tell me
Why you proceeded not against these feats,
So criminal and so capital in nature,
As by your safety, greatness, wisdom, all things else,
You mainly were stirred up.

10 **King.** O, for two special reasons,
Which may to you perhaps seem much unsinewed,
But yet to me they're strong. The Queen his mother
Lives almost by his looks, and for myself
(My virtue or my plague, be it either which),
15 She is so conjunctive to my life and soul
That, as the star moves not but in his sphere,
I could not but by her. The other motive
Why to a public count I might not go
Is the great love the general gender bear him,
20 Who, dipping all his faults in their affection,
Work like the spring that turneth wood to stone,
Convert his gyves to graces, so that my arrows,
Too slightly timbered for so loud a wind,
Would have reverted to my bow again,
25 But not where I have aimed them.

Laertes. And so have I a noble father lost,
A sister driven into desp'rate terms,
Whose worth, if praises may go back again,
Stood challenger on mount of all the age
30 For her perfections. But my revenge will come.

King. Break not your sleeps for that. You must not think
That we are made of stuff so flat and dull
That we can let our beard be shook with danger
And think it pastime. You shortly shall hear more.
35 I loved your father, and we love ourself,
And that, I hope, will teach you to imagine—

[*Enter a* Messenger *with letters.*]

How now? What news?

45 *naked:* destitute, defenseless.

50 Claudius wonders if this is a deception and no such thing has occurred.

52 *character:* handwriting.

61 *So:* as long as.

63 *checking at:* turning away from.

65 *device:* devising.

Messenger.   Letters, my lord, from Hamlet.
These to your Majesty, this to the Queen.

King. From Hamlet? Who brought them?

40 **Messenger.** Sailors, my lord, they say. I saw them not.
They were given me by Claudio. He received them
Of him that brought them.

King.   Laertes, you shall hear them.—
Leave us.

[Messenger *exits.*]

[*Reads.*] *High and mighty, you shall know I am set*
45 *naked on your kingdom. Tomorrow shall I beg*
leave to see your kingly eyes, when I shall (first
asking your pardon) thereunto recount the occasion
of my sudden and more strange return. Hamlet.
What should this mean? Are all the rest come back?
50 Or is it some abuse and no such thing?

Laertes. Know you the hand?

King. 'Tis Hamlet's character. "Naked"—
And in a postscript here, he says "alone."
Can you advise me?

55 **Laertes.** I am lost in it, my lord. But let him come.
It warms the very sickness in my heart
That I shall live and tell him to his teeth
"Thus didst thou."

King.   If it be so, Laertes
(As how should it be so? how otherwise?),
60 Will you be ruled by me?

Laertes.   Ay, my lord,
So you will not o'errule me to a peace.

King. To thine own peace. If he be now returned,
As checking at his voyage, and that he means
No more to undertake it, I will work him
65 To an exploit, now ripe in my device,

68 *uncharge the practice:* not blame the plot.

72 *organ:* agent, instrument.

75–84 The rest of Laertes's qualities combined did not inspire as much envy in Hamlet as this one, which ranks lowest in Claudius's regard. Yet this quality is important even if only a mere decoration (*very ribbon*), because light, carefree clothes (*livery*) are as well-suited to youth as more richly trimmed or sober clothes (*his sables and his weeds*) are to old age, suggesting well-being and dignity.

87 *can well:* are skillful.

90–91 *encorpsed . . . beast:* as if he and the horse shared the same body, a double-natured beast (like the mythical centaur, half man and half horse).

91–93 His feats surpassed the ability of Claudius's imagination to reconstruct them.

96 *brooch:* ornament.

Under the which he shall not choose but fall;
And for his death no wind of blame shall breathe,
But even his mother shall uncharge the practice
And call it accident.

70 **Laertes.** My lord, I will be ruled,
The rather if you could devise it so
That I might be the organ.

King.   It falls right.
You have been talked of since your travel much,
And that in Hamlet's hearing, for a quality
75 Wherein they say you shine. Your sum of parts
Did not together pluck such envy from him
As did that one, and that, in my regard,
Of the unworthiest siege.

Laertes. What part is that, my lord?

80 **King.** A very ribbon in the cap of youth—
Yet needful too, for youth no less becomes
The light and careless livery that it wears
Than settled age his sables and his weeds,
Importing health and graveness. Two months since
85 Here was a gentleman of Normandy.
I have seen myself, and served against, the French,
And they can well on horseback, but this gallant
Had witchcraft in 't. He grew unto his seat,
And to such wondrous doing brought his horse
90 As had he been encorpsed and demi-natured
With the brave beast. So far he topped my thought
That I in forgery of shapes and tricks
Come short of what he did.

Laertes.   A Norman was 't?

King. A Norman.

95 **Laertes.** Upon my life, Lamord.

King.   The very same.

Laertes. I know him well. He is the brooch indeed

98 *made confession of:* testified about.

100 *art . . . defence:* skill and practice in fencing.

103 *'scrimers:* fencers.

108 *play:* fence.

114 *begun by time:* created by circumstance.

115 *passages of proof:* actual examples.

116 *qualifies:* modifies, weakens.

118 *snuff:* the charred part of a wick that dims the candle's flame.

119 *nothing . . . still:* Nothing remains forever at the same level of goodness.

120 *pleurisy:* excess.

121 *his own too-much:* its own excess.

121–122 *That we . . . would:* If one wishes to do something, one should act while the will exists.

123 *abatements:* lessenings.

125–126 *spendthrift sigh . . . easing:* an allusion to an old belief that sighing brings momentary relief but weakens people by drawing blood from the heart.

126 *quick of th' ulcer:* the heart of the matter.

And gem of all the nation.

King. He made confession of you
And gave you such a masterly report
100   For art and exercise in your defense,
And for your rapier most especial,
That he cried out 'twould be a sight indeed
If one could match you. The 'scrimers of their nation
He swore had neither motion, guard, nor eye,
105   If you opposed them. Sir, this report of his
Did Hamlet so envenom with his envy
That he could nothing do but wish and beg
Your sudden coming-o'er, to play with you.
Now out of this—

Laertes.   What out of this, my lord?

110 **King.** Laertes, was your father dear to you?
Or are you like the painting of a sorrow,
A face without a heart?

Laertes.   Why ask you this?

King. Not that I think you did not love your father,
But that I know love is begun by time
115   And that I see, in passages of proof,
Time qualifies the spark and fire of it.
There lives within the very flame of love
A kind of wick or snuff that will abate it,
And nothing is at a like goodness still;
120   For goodness, growing to a pleurisy,
Dies in his own too-much. That we would do
We should do when we would; for this "would" changes
And hath abatements and delays as many
As there are tongues, are hands, are accidents;
125   And then this "should" is like a spendthrift sigh,
That hurts by easing. But to the quick of th' ulcer:
Hamlet comes back; what would you undertake
To show yourself indeed your father's son
More than in words?

130 ***should murder sanctuarize:*** should protect a
murderer from punishment. (In medieval times, a
criminal who took refuge, or sanctuary, in a church
could not be taken prisoner by civil authorities.)

134 ***put on those shall:*** arrange for people to.

136 ***in fine:*** finally.

137 ***remiss:*** carelessly unsuspicious.

138 ***generous:*** noble-minded

141 ***unbated:*** not blunted. (Foils used in matches are
blunted to avoid injury.); ***pass of practice:***
treacherous thrust.

144–149 Laertes bought from a quack doctor (***mountebank***) an
ointment (***unction***) so deadly that no medical dressing
(***cataplasm***), even one containing all of the powerful
medicinal herbs (***simples that have virtue***), can save
anyone scratched by it.

150 ***gall:*** injure.

153 ***fit us to our shape:*** suit our purposes.

153–155 If the plot should fail and our intentions (***drift***) are
revealed through our bungling, it would be better if
we never attempted it.

156 ***back:*** backup.

157 ***blast in proof:*** blow up while being tested
(as a gun might).

158 ***cunnings:*** skills (Laertes's and Hamlet's).

159 ***ha't:*** have it.

161 ***As:*** And you should.

Laertes.   To cut his throat i' th' church.

130 **King.** No place indeed should murder sanctuarize;
      Revenge should have no bounds. But, good Laertes,
      Will you do this? Keep close within your chamber.
      Hamlet, returned, shall know you are come home.
      We'll put on those shall praise your excellence
135   And set a double varnish on the fame
      The Frenchman gave you; bring you, in fine, together
      And wager on your heads. He, being remiss,
      Most generous, and free from all contriving,
      Will not peruse the foils, so that with ease,
140   Or with a little shuffling, you may choose
      A sword unbated, and in a pass of practice
      Requite him for your father.

Laertes.   I will do 't,
      And for that purpose I'll anoint my sword.
      I bought an unction of a mountebank
145   So mortal that, but dip a knife in it,
      Where it draws blood no cataplasm so rare,
      Collected from all simples that have virtue
      Under the moon, can save the thing from death
      That is but scratched withal. I'll touch my point
150   With this contagion, that, if I gall him slightly,
      It may be death.

King.   Let's further think of this,
      Weigh what convenience both of time and means
      May fit us to our shape. If this should fail,
      And that our drift look through our bad perform-
          ance,
155   'Twere better not assayed. Therefore this project
      Should have a back or second that might hold
      If this did blast in proof. Soft, let me see.
      We'll make a solemn wager on your cunnings—
      I ha 't!
160   When in your motion you are hot and dry
      (As make your bouts more violent to that end)
      And that he calls for drink, I'll have prepared him

163 *A chalice for the nonce:* a cup of wine for the occasion.

164 *stuck:* thrust.

169 *askant:* slanting over.

170 *his hoar:* its gray.

171 *Therewith . . . make:* she used the willow twigs to make elaborate wreaths.

172 *long purples:* orchids.

173 *liberal:* free-spoken.

174 *cold:* chaste.

175 *pendant boughs:* overhanging branches; *coronet:* made into a wreath or crown.

176 *envious sliver:* malicious branch.

180 *lauds:* hymns.

181 *incapable:* unaware.

182 *native and endued:* naturally adapted.

188–192 Although at first determined to choke back his tears, Laertes concludes that tears are a natural trait (*trick*), which shame cannot prevent. When all his tears are shed, the womanly part of him will be gone.

A chalice for the nonce, whereon but sipping,
If he by chance escape your venomed stuck,
165 Our purpose may hold there.—But stay, what noise?

[*Enter* Queen.]

Queen. One woe doth tread upon another's heel,
So fast they follow. Your sister's drowned, Laertes.

Laertes. Drowned? O, where?

Queen. There is a willow grows askant the brook
170 That shows his hoar leaves in the glassy stream.
Therewith fantastic garlands did she make
Of crowflowers, nettles, daisies, and long purples,
That liberal shepherds give a grosser name,
But our cold maids do "dead men's fingers" call them.
175 There on the pendant boughs her coronet weeds
Clamb'ring to hang, an envious sliver broke,
When down her weedy trophies and herself
Fell in the weeping brook. Her clothes spread wide,
And mermaid-like awhile they bore her up,
180 Which time she chanted snatches of old lauds,
As one incapable of her own distress
Or like a creature native and endued
Unto that element. But long it could not be
Till that her garments, heavy with their drink,
185 Pulled the poor wretch from her melodious lay
To muddy death.

Laertes.   Alas, then she is drowned.

Queen. Drowned, drowned.

Laertes. Too much of water hast thou, poor Ophelia,
And therefore I forbid my tears. But yet
190 It is our trick; nature her custom holds,
Let shame say what it will. When these are gone,
The woman will be out.—Adieu, my lord.
I have a speech o' fire that fain would blaze,
But that this folly drowns it.

[*He exits.*]

King.   Let's follow, Gertrude.
195   How much I had to do to calm his rage!
       Now fear I this will give it start again.
       Therefore, let's follow.

[*They exit.*]

1 **Christian burial:** Suicides were not allowed to be buried with Christian funeral rites. Although the previous scene suggests that Ophelia's death was an accident, rumors seem to have circulated that she killed herself.

2 **salvation:** probably a blunder for **damnation.**

4 **straight:** immediately; **crowner:** coroner; **sat on her:** held an inquest into her death; **finds it:** gave a verdict allowing.

9 **se offendendo:** a blunder for **se defendendo,** a legal term meaning "in self-defense."

12 **Argal:** a blunder for Latin **ergo,** "therefore."

13 **wittingly:** intentionally.

14 **goodman:** a title used before the name of a profession or craft; **delver:** digger.

FIVE

Scene 1 *A churchyard.*

Hamlet and Horatio enter a churchyard where a man is digging a grave. After talking to the Gravedigger, Hamlet considers how death brings everyone down to the same level. As the funeral procession approaches, he and Horatio step off to the side. Laertes grows angry at the priest, who refuses to perform a full service because he suspects that Ophelia committed suicide. He leaps into his sister's grave and curses Hamlet. Hamlet, offended by this display of mourning, insults Laertes. The two men wrestle until they are pulled apart.

[*Enter* Gravedigger *and* Another.]

Gravedigger. Is she to be buried in Christian burial, when she willfully seeks her own salvation?

Other. I tell thee she is. Therefore make her grave straight. The crowner hath sat on her and finds it
5   Christian burial.

Gravedigger. How can that be, unless she drowned herself in her own defense?

Other. Why, 'tis found so.

Gravedigger. It must be se offendendo; it cannot be else.
10   For here lies the point: if I drown myself wittingly, it argues an act, and an act hath three branches—it is to act, to do, to perform. Argal, she drowned herself wittingly.

Other. Nay, but hear you, goodman delver—

17 **will he, nill he:** willy-nilly, whether he wishes it or not.

23 **'quest:** inquest.

27 **thou sayst:** you speak the truth.

28 **count'nance:** privilege.

30 **even-Christian:** fellow Christians.

32 **hold up:** keep up.

34 **bore arms:** had a coat of arms (the sign of a gentleman).

41 **Go to:** go on (an expression of impatience).

44 **frame:** structure.

15 **Gravedigger.** Give me leave. Here lies the water; good.
Here stands the man; good. If the man go to this
water and drown himself, it is (will he, nill he) he
goes; mark you that. But if the water come to him
and drown him, he drowns not himself. Argal, he
20 that is not guilty of his own death shortens not his
own life.

Other. But is this law?

Gravedigger. Ay, marry, is 't—crowner's 'quest law.

Other. Will you ha' the truth on 't? If this had not
25 been a gentlewoman, she should have been buried
out o' Christian burial.

Gravedigger. Why, there thou sayst. And the more pity
that great folk should have count'nance in this
world to drown or hang themselves more than
30 their even-Christian. Come, my spade. There is no
ancient gentlemen but gard'ners, ditchers, and
grave-makers. They hold up Adam's profession.

Other. Was he a gentleman?

Gravedigger. He was the first that ever bore arms.

35 **Other.** Why, he had none.

Gravedigger. What, art a heathen? How dost thou
understand the scripture? The scripture says Adam
digged. Could he dig without arms? I'll put another
question to thee. If thou answerest me not to the
40 purpose, confess thyself—

Other. Go to!

Gravedigger. What is he that builds stronger than
either the mason, the shipwright, or the carpenter?

Other. The gallows-maker; for that frame outlives a
45 thousand tenants.

Gravedigger. I like thy wit well, in good faith. The gal-

48–50 *Now, thou . . . to thee:* Since you blasphemously say that the gallows is stronger than the church, you may be headed for the gallows.

53 *unyoke:* stop work for the day.

56 *Mass:* by the Mass.

57–58 The Gravedigger tells him to stop beating his brains to figure it out, because a beating won't make a slow donkey pick up its pace.

62–123 The Gravedigger sings a version of a popular Elizabethan song, with some added grunts (*O* and *a*), as he works.

68–69 *Custom . . . easiness:* Habit has made it easy for him.

71 *hath the daintier sense:* is more sensitive.

lows does well. But how does it well? It does well
to those that do ill. Now, thou dost ill to say the
gallows is built stronger than the church. Argal, the
50 gallows may do well to thee. To 't again, come.

Other. "Who builds stronger than a mason, a shipwright, or a carpenter?"

Gravedigger. Ay, tell me that, and unyoke.

Other. Marry, now I can tell.

55 **Gravedigger.** To 't.

Other. Mass, I cannot tell.

[*Enter* Hamlet *and* Horatio *afar off.*]

Gravedigger. Cudgel thy brains no more about it, for
your dull ass will not mend his pace with beating.
And, when you are asked this question next, say "a
60 grave-maker." The houses he makes lasts till doomsday. Go, get thee in, and fetch me a stoup of liquor.

[*The* Other Man *exits and the* Gravedigger *digs and sings.*]

In youth when I did love, did love,
  Methought it was very sweet
To contract—O—the time for—a—my behove,
65   *O, methought there—a—was nothing—a—meet.*

Hamlet. Has this fellow no feeling of his business? He
sings in grave-making.

Horatio. Custom hath made it in him a property of
easiness.

70 **Hamlet.** 'Tis e'en so. The hand of little employment
hath the daintier sense.

Gravedigger [*sings*].
  But age with his stealing steps
  Hath clawed me in his clutch,
  And hath shipped me into the land,
75   *As if I had never been such.*

77 *jowls:* strikes, dashes.

79–81 The skull, which the Gravedigger gets the better of, might have been the head (**pate**) of a schemer who would have tried to get the better of God.

90 *chapless:* missing the lower jaw; *mazard:* head.

91 *revolution:* turn of Fortune's wheel; *an:* if.

92 *trick:* ability.

92–94 Hamlet asks whether the cost of bringing up these people was so low that one may play a game with their bones. (The game **loggets** was played by tossing pieces of wood at a stake.)

100 *quiddities:* subtle arguments, quibbles.

101 *quillities:* subtle distinctions; *tenures:* terms for the holding of property.

103 *sconce:* head.

104–114 Hamlet lists different legal terms related to the buying and holding of property. *Fines* were documents (continued on page 246)

[He digs up a skull.]

Hamlet. That skull had a tongue in it and could sing
once. How the knave jowls it to the ground as if
'twere Cain's jawbone, that did the first murder!
This might be the pate of a politician which this
80   ass now o'erreaches, one that would circumvent
God, might it not?

Horatio. It might, my lord.

Hamlet. Or of a courtier, which could say "Good
morrow, sweet lord! How dost thou, sweet lord?"
85   This might be my Lord Such-a-one that praised my
Lord Such-a-one's horse when he went to beg it,
might it not?

Horatio. Ay, my lord.

Hamlet. Why, e'en so. And now my Lady Worm's,
90   chapless and knocked about the mazard with a
sexton's spade. Here's fine revolution, an we had
the trick to see 't. Did these bones cost no more the
breeding but to play at loggets with them? Mine
ache to think on 't.

Gravedigger. *[sings]*
95   *A pickax and a spade, a spade,*
          For and a shrouding sheet,
          O, a pit of clay for to be made
          For such a guest is meet.

[He digs up more skulls.]

Hamlet. There's another. Why may not that be the
100   skull of a lawyer? Where be his quiddities now, his
quillities, his cases, his tenures, and his tricks? Why
does he suffer this mad knave now to knock him
about the sconce with a dirty shovel and will not
tell him of his action of battery? Hum, this fellow
105   might be in 's time a great buyer of land, with his
statutes, his recognizances, his fines, his double

(**104-114** continued)
involved in the transfer of estates; Hamlet also uses the word to refer to the "end result" of the lawyer's legal work and his "elegant" head filled with "small parti- cles" of dirt. He plays similarly off the meanings of other terms, remarking that all of the lawyer's deeds (**indentures, conveyances**) and other documents will scarcely fit in the coffin, yet the lawyer is the owner (**inheritor**) of no more space than that.

119   **assurance in that:** safety in legal documents.

120   **sirrah:** a term used to address inferiors.

125   **out on't:** outside of it.

130   **quick:** living.

vouchers, his recoveries. Is this the fine of his fines
and the recovery of his recoveries, to have his fine
pate full of fine dirt? Will his vouchers vouch him
110 no more of his purchases, and double ones too,
than the length and breadth of a pair of indentures?
The very conveyances of his lands will scarcely lie
in this box, and must th' inheritor himself have no
more, ha?

115 **Horatio.** Not a jot more, my lord.

Hamlet. Is not parchment made of sheepskins?

Horatio. Ay, my lord, and of calves' skins too.

Hamlet. They are sheep and calves which seek out
assurance in that. I will speak to this fellow.—
120 Whose grave's this, sirrah?

Gravedigger. Mine, sir.
[*Sings.*] O, *a pit of clay for to be made*
For such a guest is meet.

Hamlet. I think it be thine indeed, for thou liest in 't.

125 **Gravedigger.** You lie out on 't, sir, and therefore 'tis not
yours. For my part, I do not lie in 't, yet it is mine.

Hamlet. Thou dost lie in 't, to be in 't and say it is
thine. 'Tis for the dead, not for the quick; therefore
thou liest.

130 **Gravedigger.** 'Tis a quick lie, sir; 'twill away again from
me to you.

Hamlet. What man dost thou dig it for?

Gravedigger. For no man, sir.

Hamlet. What woman then?

135 **Gravedigger.** For none, neither.

Hamlet. Who is to be buried in 't?

Gravedigger. One that was a woman, sir, but, rest her

139 *absolute:* strict, precise.

140 *by the card:* accurately; *equivocation:* use of words that are vague or have more than one meaning.

142–144 The present age has grown so refined (*picked*) that hardly any distinction remains between a peasant and a courtier; the peasant walks so closely that he chafes (*galls*) the courtier's sore heel (*kibe*).

163 *ground:* cause. (The Gravedigger takes it in the sense of "land.")

soul, she's dead.

Hamlet. How absolute the knave is! We must speak
140   by the card, or equivocation will undo us. By the
Lord, Horatio, this three years I have took note of
it: the age is grown so picked that the toe of the
peasant comes so near the heel of the courtier, he
galls his kibe.—How long hast thou been grave
145   maker?

Gravedigger. Of all the days i' th' year, I came to 't that
day that our last King Hamlet overcame Fortinbras.

Hamlet. How long is that since?

Gravedigger. Cannot you tell that? Every fool can tell
150   that. It was that very day that young Hamlet was
born—he that is mad, and sent into England?

Hamlet. Ay, marry, why was he sent into England?

Gravedigger. Why, because he was mad. He shall
recover his wits there. Or if he do not, 'tis no great
155   matter there.

Hamlet. Why?

Gravedigger. 'Twill not be seen in him there. There the
men are as mad as he.

Hamlet. How came he mad?

160 **Gravedigger.** Very strangely, they say.

Hamlet. How "strangely"?

Gravedigger. Faith, e'en with losing his wits.

Hamlet. Upon what ground?

Gravedigger. Why, here in Denmark. I have been sexton
165   here, man and boy, thirty years.

Hamlet. How long will a man lie i' th' earth ere he rot?

Gravedigger. Faith, if he be not rotten before he die

168 *pocky:* rotten, infected with syphilis.

169 *scarce hold the laying in:* barely hold together until they are buried.

174–175 *your . . . body:* Water is a terrible (*sore*) decayer of vile (*whoreson*) corpses.

175 *lien you:* lain.

193 *gibes:* taunts; *gambols:* pranks.

196 *chapfallen:* down in the mouth, missing the lower jaw.

197–198 *let her . . . come:* Even if she covers her face with an inch of makeup, eventually she will have this appearance (*favor*).

(as we have many pocky corses nowadays that will scarce hold the laying in), he will last you some eight year or nine year. A tanner will last you nine year.

Hamlet. Why he more than another?

Gravedigger. Why, sir, his hide is so tanned with his trade that he will keep out water a great while; and your water is a sore decayer of your whoreson dead body. Here's a skull now hath lien you i' th' earth three-and-twenty years.

Hamlet. Whose was it?

Gravedigger. A whoreson mad fellow's it was. Whose do you think it was?

Hamlet. Nay, I know not.

Gravedigger. A pestilence on him for a mad rogue! He poured a flagon of Rhenish on my head once. This same skull, sir, was, sir, Yorick's skull, the King's jester.

Hamlet. This?

Gravedigger. E'en that.

Hamlet [*taking the skull*]. Let me see. Alas, poor Yorick! I knew him, Horatio—a fellow of infinite jest, of most excellent fancy. He hath bore me on his back a thousand times, and now how abhorred in my imagination it is! My gorge rises at it. Here hung those lips that I have kissed I know not how oft. Where be your gibes now? your gambols? your songs? your flashes of merriment that were wont to set the table on a roar? Not one now to mock your own grinning? Quite chapfallen? Now get you to my lady's chamber, and tell her, let her paint an inch thick, to this favor she must come. Make her laugh at that.—Prithee, Horatio, tell me one thing.

Horatio. What's that, my lord?

201 *Alexander:* Alexander the Great.

208 *bunghole:* a hole in a keg or barrel for pouring liquid.

209 *curiously:* minutely, closely.

211 *modesty:* moderation.

214 *loam:* a mixture of clay, sand, and straw used for plastering.

216 *Imperious:* imperial;

219 *flaw:* gust of wind.

222 *maimèd:* incomplete.

224 *Fordo:* destroy; *some estate:* high rank.

225 *Couch . . . mark:* Let us conceal ourselves awhile and observe.

Hamlet. Dost thou think Alexander looked o' this
fashion i' th' earth?

Horatio. E'en so.

Hamlet. And smelt so? Pah!

[*He puts the skull down.*]

205   **Horatio.** E'en so, my lord.

Hamlet. To what base uses we may return, Horatio!
Why may not imagination trace the noble dust of
Alexander till he find it stopping a bunghole?

Horatio. 'Twere to consider too curiously to consider so.

210   **Hamlet.** No, faith, not a jot; but to follow him thither,
with modesty enough and likelihood to lead it, as
thus: Alexander died, Alexander was buried,
Alexander returneth to dust; the dust is earth; of
earth we make loam; and why of that loam whereto
215   he was converted might they not stop a beer barrel?
Imperious Caesar, dead and turned to clay,
Might stop a hole to keep the wind away.
O, that that earth which kept the world in awe
Should patch a wall t' expel the winter's flaw!

[*Enter* King, Queen, Laertes, Lords attendant, *and the*
corpse of Ophelia, *with a* Doctor of Divinity.]

220   But soft, but soft awhile! Here comes the King,
The Queen, the courtiers. Who is this they follow?
And with such maimèd rites? This doth betoken
The corse they follow did with desp'rate hand
Fordo its own life. 'Twas of some estate.
225   Couch we awhile and mark.

[*They step aside.*]

Laertes. What ceremony else?

Hamlet. That is Laertes, a very noble youth. Mark.

Laertes. What ceremony else?

229–233 The priest says he has performed her funeral rites to the extent allowed under church law. The manner of her death was suspicious, and if the King's orders hadn't overruled the procedures, she would have remained buried in unsanctified ground until Judgment Day.

233 *For:* instead of.

234 *Shards:* pieces of broken pottery; *should be:* would have been.

235 *virgin crants:* wreaths placed on the coffin as a sign of virginity.

236 *strewments:* flowers strewn on a grave.

236–237 *bringing . . . burial:* being laid to rest in consecrated ground with church bells tolling.

240–241 *such rest . . . souls:* pray for her to have the same rest as those who died in peace.

245 *howling:* in hell.

252–253 *thy most . . . thee of:* deprived you of your excellent mind.

257 *Pelion:* In Greek mythology, giants placed Mount Pelion on top of Mount Ossa in an attempt to reach the top of Mount Olympus, home of the gods.

Doctor. Her obsequies have been as far enlarged

230 As we have warranty. Her death was doubtful,
And, but that great command o'ersways the order,
She should in ground unsanctified been lodged
Till the last trumpet. For charitable prayers
Shards, flints, and pebbles should be thrown on her.

235 Yet here she is allowed her virgin crants,
Her maiden strewments, and the bringing home
Of bell and burial.

Laertes. Must there no more be done?

Doctor.   No more be done.
We should profane the service of the dead

240 To sing a requiem and such rest to her
As to peace-parted souls.

Laertes.   Lay her i' th' earth,
And from her fair and unpolluted flesh
May violets spring! I tell thee, churlish priest,
A minist'ring angel shall my sister be

245 When thou liest howling.

Hamlet [*to Horatio*].   What, the fair Ophelia?

Queen. Sweets to the sweet, farewell!
    She scatters flowers.
I hoped thou shouldst have been my Hamlet's wife;
I thought thy bride-bed to have decked, sweet maid,

250 And not have strewed thy grave.

Laertes.   O, treble woe
Fall ten times treble on that cursèd head
Whose wicked deed thy most ingenious sense
Deprived thee of!—Hold off the earth awhile,
Till I have caught her once more in mine arms.

[*Leaps in the grave.*]

255 Now pile your dust upon the quick and dead,
Till of this flat a mountain you have made
T' o'ertop old Pelion or the skyish head

260–262 *wand'ring stars:* planets; *wonder-wounded:* struck with amazement. *Why has Laertes's speech offended Hamlet?*

265 *splenitive:* quick-tempered.

279 *forbear him:* leave him alone.

281 *Woo't:* wilt thou.

Of blue Olympus.

Hamlet [*advancing*].　　What is he whose grief
Bears such an emphasis, whose phrase of sorrow
260　Conjures the wand'ring stars and makes them stand
Like wonder-wounded hearers? This is I,
Hamlet the Dane.

Laertes [*coming out of the grave*].
　　　　　　The devil take thy soul!

Hamlet. Thou pray'st not well.

[*They grapple.*]

I prithee take thy fingers from my throat,
265　For though I am not splenitive and rash,
Yet have I in me something dangerous,
Which let thy wisdom fear. Hold off thy hand.

King. Pluck them asunder.

Queen. Hamlet! Hamlet!

270　**All.** Gentlemen!

Horatio. Good my lord, be quiet.

[*Hamlet and Laertes are separated.*]

Hamlet. Why, I will fight with him upon this theme
Until my eyelids will no longer wag!

Queen. O my son, what theme?

275　**Hamlet.** I loved Ophelia. Forty thousand brothers
Could not with all their quantity of love
Make up my sum. What wilt thou do for her?

King. O, he is mad, Laertes!

Queen. For love of God, forbear him.

280　**Hamlet.** 'Swounds, show me what thou't do.
Woo't weep, woo't fight, woo't fast, woo't tear
　　thyself,

282 *eisel:* vinegar.

285 *quick:* alive.

288 *Singeing his . . . zone:* burning its head in the sphere of the Sun's orbit.

289 *Ossa:* See note to line 265; *an thou'lt mouth:* if you rant.

290 *mere:* utter.

292–294 Soon Hamlet will fall as silent as a dove after its twin baby birds (*couplets*) are hatched.

297–298 Hamlet seems to be suggesting that his turn will come no matter what anyone else does.

299 *wait upon:* accompany.

301 *to the present push:* into immediate action.

Woo't drink up eisel, eat a crocodile?
I'll do 't. Dost thou come here to whine?
To outface me with leaping in her grave?
285 Be buried quick with her, and so will I.
And if thou prate of mountains, let them throw
Millions of acres on us, till our ground,
Singeing his pate against the burning zone,
Make Ossa like a wart. Nay, an thou'lt mouth,
290 I'll rant as well as thou.

Queen.   This is mere madness;
And thus awhile the fit will work on him.
Anon, as patient as the female dove
When that her golden couplets are disclosed,
His silence will sit drooping.

Hamlet.   Hear you, sir,
295 What is the reason that you use me thus?
I loved you ever. But it is no matter.
Let Hercules himself do what he may,
The cat will mew, and dog will have his day.

[Hamlet *exits.*]

King. I pray thee, good Horatio, wait upon him.

[Horatio *exits.*]

300 [*To* Laertes.] Strengthen your patience in our last
        night's speech.
We'll put the matter to the present push.—
Good Gertrude, set some watch over your son.—
This grave shall have a living monument.
An hour of quiet shortly shall we see;
305 Till then in patience our proceeding be.

[*They exit.*]

1 *see the other:* hear the rest of the story.

6 *mutines:* mutineers; *bilboes:* shackles, chains.

8 *indiscretion:* hasty actions.

9 *pall:* falter; *learn:* teach.

Scene 2 *The hall of the castle.*

Hamlet tells Horatio how, after discovering Claudius's plot, he forged a letter to have the English kill Rosencrantz and Guildenstern instead of him. A courtier enters and announces that the King wants to arrange a fencing match between Hamlet and Laertes. Hamlet suspects something is wrong, but he accepts the challenge.

Hamlet wins the first two hits of the match, and the King pours a cup of wine for him. When Hamlet declines the offer, the Queen drinks the poisoned wine. As the match continues, Laertes wounds Hamlet with his poisoned sword; then, after they scuffle and accidentally exchange swords, Hamlet wounds Laertes. The Queen dies. Laertes admits that the sword and the wine were poisoned, and Hamlet uses both to kill Claudius. After Hamlet and Laertes exchange forgiveness, the latter dies. Horatio tries to drink from the poisoned cup and join Hamlet in death, but Hamlet insists that he stay alive to explain what happened. Hamlet dies. Then Fortinbras, who was named by Hamlet to succeed to the throne, arrives on his way back from Poland. Fortinbras orders a military funeral for Hamlet.

[*Enter* Hamlet *and* Horatio.]

Hamlet. So much for this, sir. Now shall you see the
    other.
    You do remember all the circumstance?

Horatio. Remember it, my lord!

Hamlet. Sir, in my heart there was a kind of fighting
5   That would not let me sleep. Methought I lay
    Worse than the mutines in the bilboes. Rashly—
    And praised be rashness for it: let us know,
    Our indiscretion sometime serves us well
    When our deep plots do pall; and that should learn

10–11 ***There's a . . . will:*** A divine power guides our destinies, despite our clumsy attempts to fashion them ourselves.

13 ***scarfed:*** wrapped.

14 ***them:*** Rosencrantz and Guildenstern.

15 ***Fingered:*** stole; ***in fine:*** finally.

20 ***Larded:*** embellished.

21 ***importing:*** concerning.

22 ***bugs . . . life:*** imaginary terrors in my remaining alive.

23 ***on the supervise:*** upon reading this; ***no leisure bated:*** without hesitation.

24 ***stay:*** wait for.

30–31 Before Hamlet had time to consider what to do, his brains started working out a plan.

33–36 Like a politician, Hamlet once considered it beneath him to write neatly (as a clerk would), but his handwriting gave him substantial service.

us

10 There's a divinity that shapes our ends,
Rough-hew them how we will—

Horatio. That is most certain.

Hamlet. Up from my cabin,
My sea-gown scarfed about me, in the dark
Groped I to find out them; had my desire,
15 Fingered their packet, and in fine withdrew
To mine own room again, making so bold
(My fears forgetting manners) to unfold
Their grand commission; where I found, Horatio,
A royal knavery—an exact command,
20 Larded with many several sorts of reasons
Importing Denmark's health and England's too,
With—ho!—such bugs and goblins in my life,
That on the supervise, no leisure bated,
No, not to stay the grinding of the ax,
25 My head should be struck off.

Horatio. Is 't possible?

Hamlet. Here's the commission. Read it at more leisure.

[*Handing him a paper.*]

But wilt thou hear now how I did proceed?

Horatio. I beseech you.

Hamlet. Being thus benetted round with villainies,
30 Or I could make a prologue to my brains,
They had begun the play. I sat me down,
Devised a new commission, wrote it fair—
I once did hold it, as our statists do,
A baseness to write fair, and labored much
35 How to forget that learning; but, sir, now
It did me yeoman's service. Wilt thou know
Th' effect of what I wrote?

Horatio. Ay, good my lord.

38 *conjuration:* request.

39 *tributary:* a nation controlled by another nation.

41 *still:* always; *wheaten garland:* symbol of peace and prosperity.

42 *stand . . . amities:* join their friendships.

43 *suchlike . . . charge:* similar legal phrases (beginning with "whereas") that have great import. (Here, as elsewhere in the speech, Hamlet ridicules official language.)

47 *shriving time:* time for confession and absolution of sins.

48 *ordinant:* controlling events.

49 *signet:* small seal.

50 *model:* likeness.

52 *Subscribed . . . impression:* signed and sealed it.

53 *changeling:* substitution. (In legends, a changeling was a fairy child substituted for a human baby.)

54 *what to this was sequent:* what followed.

58 *defeat:* destruction.

59 *insinuation:* worming their way in.

60–62 *'Tis . . . opposites:* It is dangerous for inferior people to come between the fiercely thrusting sword points of mighty antagonists.

64 *Does it . . . upon:* don't you think it is now my duty.

66 The Danish king was elected by a small group of electors. Hamlet suggests that Claudius manipulated this process to gain the throne.

67 *angle:* fishhook; *proper:* own.

68 *cozenage:* deception.

69 *quit:* pay back.

Hamlet. An earnest conjuration from the King,
    As England was his faithful tributary,
40 As love between them like the palm might flourish,
    As peace should still her wheaten garland wear
    And stand a comma 'tween their amities,
    And many suchlike ases of great charge,
    That, on the view and knowing of these contents,
45 Without debatement further, more or less,
    He should those bearers put to sudden death,
    Not shriving time allowed.

Horatio.   How was this sealed?

Hamlet. Why, even in that was heaven ordinant.
    I had my father's signet in my purse,
50 Which was the model of that Danish seal;
    Folded the writ up in the form of th' other,
    Subscribed it, gave 't th' impression, placed it safely,
    The changeling never known. Now, the next day
    Was our sea-fight; and what to this was sequent
55 Thou knowest already.

Horatio. So Guildenstern and Rosencrantz go to 't.

Hamlet. Why, man, they did make love to this
        employment.
    They are not near my conscience. Their defeat
    Does by their own insinuation grow.
60 'Tis dangerous when the baser nature comes
    Between the pass and fell incensèd points
    Of mighty opposites.

Horatio. Why, what a king is this!

Hamlet. Does it not, think thee, stand me now upon—
65 He that hath killed my king and whored my mother,
    Popped in between th' election and my hopes,
    Thrown out his angle for my proper life,
    And with such cozenage—is 't not perfect conscience
    To quit him with this arm? And is 't not to be
        damned

70–71 *come/In:* grow into.

74–75 Hamlet says that although he only has a short time in which to act, a man's life is also brief, lasting no longer than it takes to count to one. *Compare this response with his "To be or not to be" speech in Act 3, sc. 1. How would you describe his mood and thoughts in each situation?*

78 *image:* likeness.

80 *bravery:* showiness.

88–89 *Let a . . . mess:* If a man owns a lot of livestock, no matter how much he resembles them, he may eat at the king's table.

89 *chough:* chattering bird.

93–106 Men commonly wore their hats indoors but removed them in the presence of superiors. Hamlet mocks not only this show of respect but also Osric's insistence on agreeing with everything Hamlet says.

98 *indifferent:* somewhat.

70   To let this canker of our nature come
     In further evil?

Horatio. It must be shortly known to him from England
     What is the issue of the business there.

Hamlet. It will be short. The interim's mine,
75   And a man's life's no more than to say "one."
     But I am very sorry, good Horatio,
     That to Laertes I forgot myself,
     For by the image of my cause I see
     The portraiture of his. I'll court his favors.
80   But, sure, the bravery of his grief did put me
     Into a tow'ring passion.

Horatio.   Peace, who comes here?

[*Enter* Osric, *a courtier.*]

Osric. Your lordship is right welcome back to Denmark.

Hamlet. I humbly thank you, sir. [*Aside to* Horatio.]
     Dost know this waterfly?

85   **Horatio** [*aside to* Hamlet]. No, my good lord.

Hamlet [*aside to* Horatio]. Thy state is the more gracious,
     for 'tis a vice to know him. He hath much land,
     and fertile. Let a beast be lord of beasts and his
     crib shall stand at the king's mess. 'Tis a chough,
90   but, as I say, spacious in the possession of dirt.

Osric. Sweet lord, if your lordship were at leisure, I
     should impart a thing to you from his Majesty.

Hamlet. I will receive it, sir, with all diligence of spirit.
     Put your bonnet to his right use: 'tis for the head.

95   **Osric.** I thank your lordship; it is very hot.

Hamlet. No, believe me, 'tis very cold; the wind is
     northerly.

Osric. It is indifferent cold, my lord, indeed.

100 *complexion:* temperament.

110–112 Among his compliments, Osric calls Laertes the map or guide (***card or calendar***) of good breeding, one who contains in him (***the continent of***) all the qualities a gentleman would look for.

113–121 Hamlet, mocking Osric's flowery speech, says that nothing has been lost in Osric's definition of Laertes, but the calculations needed to make an inventory of Laertes's excellences would be dizzying, and even then one would fail to capture him. He goes on to say that the only true likeness (***semblable***) of Laertes is his reflection in a mirror, and anyone who wanted to copy him would be nothing more than his shadow (***umbrage***).

123–124 Hamlet asks why they are speaking about Laertes.

128 ***What imports . . . of:*** for what purpose are you mentioning.

Hamlet. But yet methinks it is very sultry and hot for
my complexion.

Osric. Exceedingly, my lord; it is very sultry, as
'twere—I cannot tell how. My lord, his Majesty
bade me signify to you that he has laid a great
wager on your head. Sir, this is the matter—

Hamlet. I beseech you, remember.

[*He motions to* Osric *to put on his hat.*]

Osric. Nay, good my lord, for my ease, in good faith.
Sir, here is newly come to court Laertes—believe
me, an absolute gentleman, full of most excellent
differences, of very soft society and great showing.
Indeed, to speak feelingly of him, he is the card or
calendar of gentry, for you shall find in him the
continent of what part a gentleman would see.

Hamlet. Sir, his definement suffers no perdition in you,
though I know to divide him inventorially would
dozy th' arithmetic of memory, and yet but yaw
neither, in respect of his quick sail. But, in the verity
of extolment, I take him to be a soul of great article,
and his infusion of such dearth and rareness as, to
make true diction of him, his semblable is his mirror, and who else would trace him, his umbrage,
nothing more.

Osric. Your lordship speaks most infallibly of him.

Hamlet. The concernancy, sir? Why do we wrap the
gentleman in our more rawer breath?

Osric. Sir?

Horatio [*aside to* Hamlet]. Is 't not possible to understand in another tongue? You will to 't, sir, really.

Hamlet [*to* Osric]. What imports the nomination of this
gentleman?

Osric. Of Laertes?

131 *all 's:* all his.

136 *approve:* commend.

142–143 In the reputation (*imputation*) others have given him, his merit (*meed*) is unmatched.

145 *Rapier and dagger:* a type of fencing with a rapier (sword) held in the right hand and a dagger in the left.

147–153 Against Claudius's wager, Laertes has staked (*inpawned*) six rapiers and daggers (*poniards*), along with their accessories (*assigns*), such as straps (*hangers*) to hold the swords onto a sword belt (*girdle*), and so forth. Three of the hangers are fancifully designed (*dear to fancy*), well adjusted (*responsive*), finely crafted (*delicate*), and have an elaborate (*liberal*) design. (*Carriages,* an affected word for *hangers,* normally refers to the wheeled bases of cannons. See lines 167–173.)

155–156 Horatio jokes that he knew Hamlet would seek explanation in a marginal note.

Horatio [*aside*]. His purse is empty already; all 's golden words are spent.

Hamlet. Of him, sir.

Osric. I know you are not ignorant—

135 **Hamlet.** I would you did, sir. Yet, in faith, if you did, it would not much approve me. Well, sir?

Osric. You are not ignorant of what excellence Laertes is—

Hamlet. I dare not confess that, lest I should compare
140 with him in excellence. But to know a man well were to know himself.

Osric. I mean, sir, for his weapon. But in the imputation laid on him by them, in his meed he's unfellowed.

Hamlet. What's his weapon?

145 **Osric.** Rapier and dagger.

Hamlet. That's two of his weapons. But, well—

Osric. The King, sir, hath wagered with him six Barbary horses, against the which he has impawned, as I take it, six French rapiers and poniards, with their
150 assigns, as girdle, hangers, and so. Three of the carriages, in faith, are very dear to fancy, very responsive to the hilts, most delicate carriages, and of very liberal conceit.

Hamlet. What call you the "carriages"?

155 **Horatio** [*aside to* Hamlet]. I knew you must be edified by the margent ere you had done.

Osric. The carriages, sir, are the hangers.

Hamlet. The phrase would be more germane to the matter if we could carry a cannon by our sides. I
160 would it might be "hangers" till then. But on. Six Barbary horses against six French swords, their

165 *laid:* wagered.

166 *passes;* bouts, exchanges; *him:* Laertes.

167–168 *twelve for nine:* This phrase seems to contradict the wager that Laertes must win 8 out of 12.

169 *vouchsafe the answer:* accept the challenge. (Hamlet takes this phrase literally and asks what will happen if he gives no answer.)

174 *breathing time of day:* usual time for exercise.

175 *foils:* swords with blunt tips.

182 *commend:* present to your favor (part of a conventional phrase, but Hamlet plays off another meaning, remarking that Osric had better praise himself, because no one else would do it for him).

185 *lapwing:* A bird that supposedly left its nest soon after hatching and ran around with its shell on its head—probably a reference to Osric's hat. *What do you think is the effect of the humor included in this scene with Osric?*

187–194 After joking that Osric paid courtesies to his nurse's or mother's nipple before nursing, Hamlet complains that Osric and his type, popular in this worthless age, have only picked up a fashionable manner of speaking (*the tune of the time*) and a frothy collection of phrases that help them move through refined society (*fanned and winnowed opinions*), but the bubbles burst as soon as they are tested.

assigns, and three liberal-conceited carriages—
that's the French bet against the Danish. Why is
this all "impawned," as you call it?

165 **Osric.** The King, sir, hath laid, sir, that in a dozen
passes between yourself and him, he shall not
exceed you three hits. He hath laid on twelve for
nine, and it would come to immediate trial if your
lordship would vouchsafe the answer.

170 **Hamlet.** How if I answer no?

Osric. I mean, my lord, the opposition of your person
in trial.

Hamlet. Sir, I will walk here in the hall. If it please his
Majesty, it is the breathing time of day with me.
175 Let the foils be brought, the gentleman willing, and
the King hold his purpose, I will win for him, an I
can. If not, I will gain nothing but my shame and
the odd hits.

Osric. Shall I deliver you e'en so?

180 **Hamlet.** To this effect, sir, after what flourish your
nature will.

Osric. I commend my duty to your lordship.

Hamlet. Yours. [Osric *exits.*] He does well to commend
it himself. There are no tongues else for 's turn.

185 **Horatio.** This lapwing runs away with the shell on his
head.

Hamlet. He did comply, sir, with his dug before he
sucked it. Thus has he (and many more of the same
breed that I know the drossy age dotes on) only
190 got the tune of the time, and, out of an habit of
encounter, a kind of yeasty collection, which carries
them through and through the most fanned and
winnowed opinions; and do but blow them to their
trial, the bubbles are out.

201–202 *If his . . . whensoever:* I am ready at his convenience.

205 *In happy time:* a polite phrase of welcome.

206–207 *use some gentle entertainment:* show some
courtesy.

215–216 *gaingiving:* misgiving.

218 *repair:* coming.

219–224 Hamlet rejects *augury* (attempting to foresee the
future by interpreting omens) and declares that since
the death of even a sparrow is not left to chance, he is
ready to accept any circumstances he encounters; his
death will come sooner or later. He concludes that since
man knows nothing about the life he leaves behind,
what does it matter if he leaves early?

[*Enter a* Lord.]

195 **Lord.** My lord, his Majesty commended him to you by
young Osric, who brings back to him that you
attend him in the hall. He sends to know if your
pleasure hold to play with Laertes, or that you will
take longer time.

200 **Hamlet.** I am constant to my purposes. They follow
the King's pleasure. If his fitness speaks, mine is
ready now or whensoever, provided I be so able as
now.

Lord. The King and Queen and all are coming down.

205 **Hamlet.** In happy time.

Lord. The Queen desires you to use some gentle entertainment to Laertes before you fall to play.

Hamlet. She well instructs me.

[Lord *exits.*]

Horatio. You will lose, my lord.

210 **Hamlet.** I do not think so. Since he went into France, I
have been in continual practice. I shall win at the
odds; but thou wouldst not think how ill all's here
about my heart. But it is no matter.

Horatio. Nay, good my lord—

215 **Hamlet.** It is but foolery, but it is such a kind of gaingiving as would perhaps trouble a woman.

Horatio. If your mind dislike anything, obey it. I will
forestall their repair hither and say you are not fit.

Hamlet. Not a whit. We defy augury. There is a special
220 providence in the fall of a sparrow. If it be now, 'tis
not to come; if it be not to come, it will be now; if
it be not now, yet it will come. The readiness is all.
Since no man of aught he leaves knows, what is 't
to leave betimes? Let be.

227 *presence:* royal assembly.

229 *sore distraction:* severe confusion.
230 *exception:* disapproval.

237 *faction:* party.

240 *purposed evil:* intentional harm.

242 *That I have:* as if I had.

244–250 Laertes says that he is satisfied in regard to his own
feelings (*nature*), but in regard to his honor he will
wait until men experienced in such matters have given
their authoritative judgment (*voice and precedent*) in
favor of reconciliation, which would allow him to keep
his reputation undamaged (*name ungored*).

[*A table prepared. Enter Trumpets, Drums, and* Officers *with cushions,* King, Queen, Osric, *and all the state, foils, daggers, flagons of wine, and* Laertes.]

225 **King.** Come, Hamlet, come and take this hand from me.

[*He puts* Laertes' *hand into* Hamlet's.]

Hamlet [*to* Laertes]. Give me your pardon, sir. I have
    done you wrong;
  But pardon 't as you are a gentleman. This presence
    knows,
  And you must needs have heard, how I am punished
  With a sore distraction. What I have done
230 That might your nature, honor, and exception
  Roughly awake, I here proclaim was madness.
  Was 't Hamlet wronged Laertes? Never Hamlet.
  If Hamlet from himself be ta'en away,
  And when he's not himself does wrong Laertes,
235 Then Hamlet does it not; Hamlet denies it.
  Who does it, then? His madness. If 't be so,
  Hamlet is of the faction that is wronged;
  His madness is poor Hamlet's enemy.
  Sir, in this audience
240 Let my disclaiming from a purposed evil
  Free me so far in your most generous thoughts
  That I have shot my arrow o'er the house
  And hurt my brother.

Laertes. I am satisfied in nature,
245 Whose motive in this case should stir me most
  To my revenge; but in my terms of honor
  I stand aloof and will no reconcilement
  Till by some elder masters of known honor
  I have a voice and precedent of peace
250 To keep my name ungored. But till that time
  I do receive your offered love like love
  And will not wrong it.

Hamlet.   I embrace it freely

253 *frankly:* without any hard feelings.

255 *foil:* metallic background used to display a jewel (punning on **foils,** referring to the blunted swords).

257 *Stick fiery off:* stand out brilliantly.

260–261 Hamlet comments that Claudius has bet on (*laid the odds o'*) the weaker fencer. Claudius expresses confidence in Hamlet, but says he has arranged a handicap (*odds*) for Laertes because he has improved.

265 *likes me:* pleases me; *have all a length:* are all the same length.

269 *quit . . . exchange:* gets back at Laertes by scoring the third hit.

272 *union:* pearl.

275 *kettle:* kettledrum.

And will this brothers' wager frankly play.—
Give us the foils. Come on.

Laertes.   Come, one for me.

255 **Hamlet.** I'll be your foil, Laertes; in mine ignorance
    Your skill shall, like a star i' th' darkest night,
    Stick fiery off indeed.

Laertes.   You mock me, sir.

Hamlet. No, by this hand.

King. Give them the foils, young Osric. Cousin Hamlet,
260   You know the wager?

Hamlet.   Very well, my lord.
    Your Grace has laid the odds o' th' weaker side.

King. I do not fear it; I have seen you both.
    But, since he is better, we have therefore odds.

Laertes. This is too heavy. Let me see another.

265 **Hamlet.** This likes me well. These foils have all a length?

Osric. Ay, my good lord.

[*Prepare to play.*]

King. Set me the stoups of wine upon that table.—
    If Hamlet give the first or second hit
    Or quit in answer of the third exchange,
270   Let all the battlements their ordnance fire.
    The King shall drink to Hamlet's better breath,
    And in the cup an union shall he throw,
    Richer than that which four successive kings
    In Denmark's crown have worn. Give me the cups,
275   And let the kettle to the trumpet speak,
    The trumpet to the cannoneer without,
    The cannons to the heavens, the heaven to earth,
    "Now the King drinks to Hamlet." Come, begin.
    And you, the judges, bear a wary eye.

[*Trumpets the while.*]

292 *fat:* sweaty, out of shape.

293 *napkin:* handkerchief.

280 **Hamlet.** Come on, sir.

Laertes. Come, my lord.

[*They play.*]

Hamlet. One.

Laertes. No.

Hamlet. Judgment!

285 **Osric.** A hit, a very palpable hit.

Laertes. Well, again.

King. Stay, give me drink.—Hamlet, this pearl is thine.
　　Here's to thy health.

[*He drinks and then drops the pearl in the cup. Drum,
trumpets, and shot.*]

　　　　　　　　　　　　Give him the cup.

Hamlet. I'll play this bout first. Set it by awhile.
290　　Come. They play. Another hit. What say you?

Laertes. A touch, a touch. I do confess 't.

King. Our son shall win.

Queen.　　　　　　　He's fat and scant of breath.
　　Here, Hamlet, take my napkin; rub thy brows.
　　The Queen carouses to thy fortune, Hamlet.

[*She lifts the cup.*]

295 **Hamlet.** Good madam.

King. Gertrude, do not drink.

Queen. I will, my lord; I pray you pardon me.

[*She drinks.*]

King [*aside*]. It is the poisoned cup. It is too late.

Hamlet. I dare not drink yet, madam—by and by.

304 *pass:* thrust.

305 *make a wanton of me:* indulge me as if I were a spoiled child.

314 Laertes says he's been caught like a *woodcock* (a proverbially stupid bird) in his own trap.

300 **Queen.** Come, let me wipe thy face.

Laertes [*to* Claudius]. My lord, I'll hit him now.

King.   I do not think 't.

Laertes [*aside*]. And yet it is almost against my con-
       science.

Hamlet. Come, for the third, Laertes. You do but dally.
       I pray you pass with your best violence.
305   I am afeard you make a wanton of me.

Laertes. Say you so? Come on. [*Play.*]

Osric. Nothing neither way.

Laertes. Have at you now!

[Laertes *wounds* Hamlet. *Then in scuffling they change
rapiers, and* Hamlet *wounds* Laertes.]

King. Part them. They are incensed.

310 **Hamlet.** Nay, come again.

[*The* Queen *falls.*]

Osric. Look to the Queen there, ho!

Horatio. They bleed on both sides.—How is it, my lord?

Osric. How is 't, Laertes?

Laertes. Why as a woodcock to mine own springe,
       Osric.

[*He falls.*]

315   I am justly killed with mine own treachery.

Hamlet. How does the Queen?

King.   She swoons to see them bleed.

Queen. No, no, the drink, the drink! O, my dear
       Hamlet!
       The drink, the drink! I am poisoned. [*She dies.*]

325 *unbated:* not blunted; *practice:* trick.

333 *union:* a pun on the meanings "pearl" and "marriage." (Claudius is joining his wife in death.)

335 *tempered:* mixed.

342 *mutes:* silent observers (literally, actors without speaking parts).

343 *fell sergeant:* cruel arresting officer.

Hamlet. O villainy! Ho! Let the door be locked.

[Osric *exits.*]

320   Treachery! Seek it out.

Laertes. It is here, Hamlet. Hamlet, thou art slain.
No med'cine in the world can do thee good.
In thee there is not half an hour's life.
The treacherous instrument is in thy hand,
325   Unbated and envenomed. The foul practice
Hath turned itself on me. Lo, here I lie,
Never to rise again. Thy mother's poisoned.
I can no more. The King, the King's to blame.

Hamlet. The point envenomed too! Then, venom, to
thy work. [*Hurts the* King.]
330   All Treason, treason!

King. O, yet defend me, friends! I am but hurt.

Hamlet. Here, thou incestuous, murd'rous, damnèd
Dane,
Drink off this potion. Is thy union here?

[*Forcing him to drink the poison.*]

Follow my mother.

[King *dies.*]

Laertes.   He is justly served.
335   It is a poison tempered by himself.
Exchange forgiveness with me, noble Hamlet.
Mine and my father's death come not upon thee,
Nor thine on me.

[*Dies.*]

Hamlet. Heaven make thee free of it. I follow thee.—
340   I am dead, Horatio.—Wretched queen, adieu.—
You that look pale and tremble at this chance,
That are but mutes or audience to this act,
Had I but time (as this fell sergeant, Death,

348 *more an antique Roman:* a reference to the Roman idea that suicide can be an honorable action following a defeat or the death of a loved one.

354 *Absent thee from felicity:* deny yourself the pleasure of death.

357–359 Fortinbras, returning triumphant from Poland, has saluted the English ambassadors with a volley of gunfire.

360 *o'ercrows:* triumphs over (like the winner in a cockfight).

362–363 Hamlet predicts that Fortinbras will be elected the new Danish king and gives him his vote (**voice**). *Do you agree with Hamlet's choice?*

364 *occurrents:* occurrences.

365 *solicited:* prompted, brought about. (Hamlet dies before finishing this thought.)

Is strict in his arrest), O, I could tell you—
345 But let it be.—Horatio, I am dead.
Thou livest; report me and my cause aright
To the unsatisfied.

Horatio.   Never believe it.
I am more an antique Roman than a Dane.
Here's yet some liquor left.

[*He picks up the cup.*]

Hamlet.   As thou'rt a man,
350 Give me the cup. Let go! By heaven, I'll ha 't.
O God, Horatio, what a wounded name,
Things standing thus unknown, shall I leave behind
    me!
If thou didst ever hold me in thy heart,
Absent thee from felicity awhile
355 And in this harsh world draw thy breath in pain
To tell my story.

[*A march afar off and shot within.*]

                    What warlike noise is this?

[*Enter Osric.*]

Osric. Young Fortinbras, with conquest come from
    Poland,
To th' ambassadors of England gives
This warlike volley.

Hamlet.   O, I die, Horatio!
360 The potent poison quite o'ercrows my spirit.
I cannot live to hear the news from England.
But I do prophesy th' election lights
On Fortinbras; he has my dying voice.
So tell him, with th' occurrents, more and less,
365 Which have solicited—the rest is silence.
O, O, O, O!

[*Dies.*]

373 This heap of dead bodies (*quarry*) proclaims a massacre (*cries on havoc*).

374 *toward:* in preparation.

381 *his:* Claudius's.

384 *so jump upon this bloody question:* so soon after this bloody quarrel.

387 *stage:* platform.

390 *carnal, bloody, and unnatural acts:* Claudius's murder of his brother and marriage to Gertrude.

391 *accidental judgments, casual slaughters:* punishments that occurred by chance.

392 *put on:* instigated; *forced:* contrived.

Horatio. Now cracks a noble heart. Good night, sweet
    prince,
And flights of angels sing thee to thy rest.

[*March within.*]

Why does the drum come hither?

[*Enter* Fortinbras *with the* English Ambassadors *with*
Drum, Colors, and Attendants.]

370 **Fortinbras.** Where is this sight?

Horatio. What is it you would see?
If aught of woe or wonder, cease your search.

Fortinbras. This quarry cries on havoc. O proud Death,
What feast is toward in thine eternal cell
375 That thou so many princes at a shot
So bloodily hast struck?

Ambassador.   The sight is dismal,
And our affairs from England come too late.
The ears are senseless that should give us hearing
To tell him his commandment is fulfilled,
380 That Rosencrantz and Guildenstern are dead.
Where should we have our thanks?

Horatio.   Not from his mouth,
Had it th' ability of life to thank you.
He never gave commandment for their death.
But since, so jump upon this bloody question,
385 You from the Polack wars, and you from England,
Are here arrived, give order that these bodies
High on a stage be placed to the view,
And let me speak to th' yet unknowing world
How these things came about. So shall you hear
390 Of carnal, bloody, and unnatural acts,
Of accidental judgments, casual slaughters,
Of deaths put on by cunning and forced cause,
And, in this upshot, purposes mistook
Fall'n on th' inventors' heads. All this can I

395 *deliver:* tell the story of.

398–399 Fortinbras says he has some unforgotten claims to Denmark, and this is a favorable time to present them.

401 *from his mouth . . . more:* the words of Hamlet, whose decision will influence other votes.

402 *presently:* immediately.

403–404 *lest more . . . happen:* lest other trouble occur in addition to these plots and accidents.

406 *put on:* enthroned, and so put to the test.

407 *passage:* death.

411 *field:* field of battle.

395   Truly deliver.

    Fortinbras.   Let us haste to hear it
    And call the noblest to the audience.
    For me, with sorrow I embrace my fortune.
    I have some rights of memory in this kingdom,
    Which now to claim my vantage doth invite me.

400   **Horatio.** Of that I shall have also cause to speak,
    And from his mouth whose voice will draw on more.
    But let this same be presently performed
    Even while men's minds are wild, lest more mischance
    On plots and errors happen.

    Fortinbras.   Let four captains
405   Bear Hamlet like a soldier to the stage,
    For he was likely, had he been put on,
    To have proved most royal; and for his passage,
    The soldier's music and the rite of war
    Speak loudly for him.
410   Take up the bodies. Such a sight as this
    Becomes the field but here shows much amiss.
    Go, bid the soldiers shoot.

    [*They exit, marching, after the which a peal of ordnance are shot off.*]

Related Readings

CONTENTS

from Introduction to *Hamlet*

by David Bevington

Since it was first written, Hamlet *has been interpreted in many different ways by actors and directors as well as by scholars. In this critical essay, 20th-century critic David Bevington offers his views of the characters and conflicts in the play.*

Hamlet, his mind attuned to philosophical matters, is keenly and poetically aware of humanity's fallen condition. He is, moreover, a shrewd observer of the Danish court, one familiar with its ways and at the same time newly returned from abroad, looking at Denmark with a stranger's eyes. What particularly darkens his view of humanity, however, is not the general fact of corrupted human nature but rather Hamlet's knowledge of a dreadful secret. Even before he learns of his father's murder, Hamlet senses that there is something more deeply amiss than his mother's overhasty marriage to her deceased husband's brother. This is serious enough, to be sure, for it violates a taboo (parallel to the marriage of a widower to his deceased wife's sister, long regarded as incestuous by the English) and is thus understandably referred to as "incest" by Hamlet and his father's ghost. The appalling spectacle of Gertrude's "wicked speed, to post / With such dexterity to incestuous sheets" (1.2.156–157) overwhelms Hamlet with revulsion at carnal appetite and intensifies the emotional crisis any son would go through when forced to contemplate his father's death and his mother's remarriage. Still, the Ghost's revelation is of something far worse, something Hamlet has subconsciously feared and suspected. "O my prophetic soul! My uncle!" (1.5.42). Now Hamlet has confirming evidence for his intuition that the world itself is "an unweeded garden / That grows to seed. Things rank and gross in nature / Possess it merely" (1.2.135–137).

Something is indeed rotten in the state of Denmark. The monarch on whom the health and safety of the kingdom depend is a murderer. Yet few persons know his secret: Hamlet, Horatio only belatedly, Claudius himself, and ourselves as audience. Many ironies and misunderstandings of the play cannot be understood without a proper awareness of this gap between Hamlet's knowledge and most others' ignorance of the murder. For, according to their own lights, Polonius and the rest behave as courtiers normally behave, obeying and flattering a king whom they acknowledge as their legitimate ruler. Hamlet, for his part, is so obsessed with the secret murder that he overreacts to those around him, rejecting overtures of friendship and becoming embittered, callous, brutal, and even violent. His antisocial behavior gives the others good reason to fear him as a menace to the state. Nevertheless, we share with Hamlet a knowledge of the truth and know that he is right, whereas the others are at best unhappily deceived by their own blind complicity in evil.

Rosencrantz and Guildenstern, for instance, are boyhood friends of Hamlet but are now dependent on the favor of King Claudius. Despite their seeming concern for their one-time comrade, and Hamlet's initial pleasure in receiving them, they are faceless courtiers whose very names, like their personalities, are virtually interchangeable. "Thanks, Rosencrantz and gentle Guildenstern," says the King, and "Thanks, Guildenstern and gentle Rosencrantz," echoes the Queen (2.2.33–34). They cannot understand why Hamlet increasingly mocks their overtures of friendship, whereas Hamlet cannot stomach their subservience to the King. The secret murder divides Hamlet from them, since only he knows of it. As the confrontation between Hamlet and Claudius grows more deadly, Rosencrantz and Guildenstern, not knowing the true cause, can only interpret Hamlet's behavior as dangerous madness. The wild display he puts on during the performance of "The Murder of Gonzago" and the killing of Polonius are evidence of a treasonous threat to the crown, eliciting from them staunch assertions of the divine right of kings. "Most holy and religious fear it is / To keep those many many bodies safe / That live and feed upon Your Majesty," professes Guildenstern, and Rosencrantz reiterates the theme: "The cess of majesty / Dies not alone, but like a gulf doth draw / What's near it with it" (3.3.8–17). These sentiments of Elizabethan orthodoxy, similar to ones frequently heard in Shakespeare's history plays, are here undercut by a devastating irony, since they are spoken unwittingly in defense of a murderer. This irony pursues Rosencrantz and Guildenstern to their graves, for they are killed performing what they see as their duty to convey Hamlet safely to England. They are as ignorant of Claudius's secret orders for the murder of Hamlet in England as they are of Claudius's real reason for wishing to be rid of his stepson. That Hamlet should ingeniously remove the secret commission from Rosencrantz and Guildenstern's packet and substitute an order for their execution is ironically fitting, even though they are guiltless of having plotted Hamlet's death. "Why, man, they did make love to this employment," says Hamlet to

Horatio. "They are not near my conscience. Their defeat / Does by their own insinuation grow" (5.2.57–59). They have condemned themselves, in Hamlet's eyes, by interceding officiously in deadly affairs of which they had no comprehension. Hamlet's judgment of them is harsh, and he himself appears hardened and pitiless in his role as agent in their deaths, but he is right that they have courted their own destiny.

Polonius, too, dies for meddling. It seems an unfair fate, since he wishes no physical harm to Hamlet, and is only trying to ingratiate himself with Claudius. Yet Polonius's complicity in jaded court politics is deeper than his fatuous parental sententiousness might lead one to suppose. His famous advice to his son, often quoted out of context as though it were wise counsel, is in fact a worldly gospel of self-interest and concern for appearances. Like his son, Laertes, he cynically presumes that Hamlet's affection for Ophelia cannot be serious, since princes are not free to marry ladies of the court; accordingly, Polonius obliges his daughter to return the love letters she so cherishes. Polonius's spies are everywhere, seeking to entrap Polonius's own son in fleshly sin or to discover symptoms of Hamlet's presumed lovesickness. Polonius may cut a ridiculous figure as a prattling busybody, but he is wily and even menacing in his intent. He has actually helped Claudius to the throne and is an essential instrument of royal policy. His ineffectuality and ignorance of the murder do not really excuse his guilty involvement.

Ophelia is more innocent than her father and brother, and more truly affectionate toward Hamlet. She earns our sympathy because she is caught between the conflicting wills of the men who are supremely important to her—her lover, her father, her brother. Obedient by instinct and training to patriarchal instruction, she is unprepared to cope with divided authority and so takes refuge in passivity. Nevertheless her pitiable story suggests that weak-willed acquiescence is poisoned by the evil to which it surrenders. However passively, Ophelia becomes an instrument through which Claudius attempts to spy on Hamlet. She is much like Gertrude, for the Queen has yielded to Claudius's importunity without ever knowing fully what awful price Claudius has paid for her and for the throne. The resemblance between Ophelia and Gertrude confirms Hamlet's tendency to generalize about feminine weakness—"frailty, thy name is woman" (1.2.146)—and prompts his misogynistic outburst against Ophelia when he concludes she, too, is spying on him. His rejection of love and friendship (except for Horatio's) seems paranoid in character and yet is at least partially justified by the fact that so many of the court are in fact conspiring to learn what he is up to.

Their oversimplification of his dilemma and their facile analyses vex Hamlet as much as their meddling. When they presume to diagnose his malady, the courtiers actually reveal more about themselves than about Hamlet—something we as readers and viewers might well bear in mind. Rosencrantz and Guildenstern think in political terms, reflecting their own ambitious natures, and Hamlet takes mordant delight in leading them on. "Sir, I lack advancement," he mockingly answers Rosencrantz's questioning as to the cause of his distemper. Rosencrantz is immediately taken in: "How can that be, when you have the voice of the King himself for your succession in Denmark?" (3.2.338–341). Actually Hamlet does hold a grudge against Claudius for having "Popped in between th' election and my hopes" (5.2.65) by using the Danish custom of "election" by the chief lords of the realm to deprive young Hamlet of the succession that would normally have been his. Nevertheless, it is a gross oversimplification to suppose that political frustration is the key to Hamlet's sorrow, and to speculate thus is presumptuous. "Why, look you now, how unworthy a thing you make of me!" Hamlet protests to Rosencrantz and Guildenstern. "You would play upon me, you would seem to know my stops, you would pluck out the heart of my mystery" (3.2.362–365). Yet the worst offender in these distortions of complex truth is Polonius, whose diagnosis of lovesickness appears to have been inspired by recollections of Polonius's own far-off youth. ("Truly in my youth I suffered much extremity for love, very near this," 2.2.189–191.) Polonius's fatuous complacency in his own powers of analysis—"If circumstances lead me, I will find / Where truth is hid, though it were hid indeed / Within the center" (2.2.157–159)—reads like a parody of Hamlet's struggle to discover what is true and what is not.

Thus, although Hamlet may seem to react with excessive bitterness toward those who are set to watch over him, the corruption he decries in Denmark is both real and universal. "The time is out of joint," he laments. "O cursèd spite / That ever I was born to set it right!" (1.5.197–198). How is he to proceed in setting things right? Ever since the nineteenth century it has been fashionable to discover reasons for Hamlet's delaying his revenge. The basic Romantic approach is to find a defect, or tragic flaw, in Hamlet himself. In Coleridge's words, Hamlet suffers from "an overbalance in the contemplative faculty" and is "one who vacillates from sensibility and procrastinates from thought, and loses the power of action in the energy of resolve." More recent psychological critics, such as Freud's disciple Ernest Jones, still seek answers to the Romantics' question by explaining Hamlet's failure of will. In Jones's interpretation, Hamlet is the victim of an Oedipal trauma; he has longed unconsciously to possess his mother and for that very reason cannot bring himself to punish the hated uncle who has supplanted him in his incestuous and forbidden desire. Such interpretations suggest, among other things, that Hamlet continues to serve as a mirror in which analysts who would pluck out the heart of his mystery see an image of their own concerns—just as Rosencrantz and Guildenstern read politics, and Polonius lovesickness, into Hamlet's distress.

We can ask, however, not only whether the explanations for Hamlet's supposed delay are valid but whether the question they seek to answer is itself valid. Is the delay unnecessary or excessive? The question did not even arise until the nineteenth century. Earlier audiences were evidently satisfied that Hamlet must test the Ghost's credibility, since apparitions can tell half-truths to deceive men, and that once Hamlet has confirmed the Ghost's word, he proceeds as resolutely as his canny adversary allows. More recent criticism, perhaps reflecting a modern absorption in existentialist philosophy, has proposed that Hamlet's dilemma is a matter not of personal failure but of the absurdity of action itself in a corrupt world. Does what Hamlet is asked to do make any sense, given the bestial nature of man and the impossibility of knowing what is right? In part it is a matter of style: Claudius's Denmark is crassly vulgar, and to combat this vulgarity on its own terms seems to require the sort of bad histrionics Hamlet derides in actors who mouth their lines or tear a passion to tatters. Hamlet's dilemma of action can best be studied in the play by comparing him with various characters who are obliged to act in situations similar to his own and who respond in meaningfully different ways.

Three young men—Hamlet, Laertes, and

Fortinbras—are called upon to avenge their fathers' violent deaths. Ophelia, too, has lost a father by violent means, and her madness and death are another kind of reaction to such a loss. The responses of Laertes and Fortinbras offer implicit lessons to Hamlet, and in both cases the lesson seems to be of the futility of positive and forceful action. Laertes thinks he has received an unambiguous mandate to revenge, since Hamlet has undoubtedly slain Polonius and helped to deprive Ophelia of her sanity. Accordingly Laertes comes back to Denmark in a fury, stirring the rabble with his demagoguery and spouting Senecan rant about dismissing conscience "to the profoundest pit" in his quest for vengeance (4.5.135). When Claudius asks what Laertes would do to Hamlet "To show yourself in deed your father's son / More than in words," Laertes fires back: "To cut his throat i' the church" (4.7.126–127). This resolution is understandable. The pity is, however, that Laertes has only superficially identified the murderer in the case. He is too easily deceived by Claudius because he has accepted easy and fallacious conclusions, and so is doomed to become a pawn in Claudius's sly maneuverings. Too late he sees his error and must die for it, begging and receiving Hamlet's forgiveness. Before we accuse Hamlet of thinking too deliberately before acting, we must consider that Laertes does not think enough.

Fortinbras of Norway, as his name implies ("strong in arms"), is one who believes in decisive action. At the beginning of the play we learn that his father has been slain in battle by old Hamlet, and that Fortinbras has collected an army to win back by force the territory fairly won by the Danes in that encounter. Like Hamlet, young Fortinbras does not succeed his father to the throne, but must now contend with an uncle-king. When this uncle, at Claudius's instigation, forbids Fortinbras to march against the Danes, and rewards him for his restraint with a huge annual income and a commission to fight the Poles instead, Fortinbras sagaciously welcomes the new opportunity. He pockets the money, marches against Poland, and waits for occasion to deliver Denmark as well into his hands. Clearly this is more of a success story than that of Laertes, and Hamlet does after all give his blessing to the "election" of Fortinbras to the Danish throne. Fortinbras is the man of the hour, the representative of a restored political stability. Yet Hamlet's admiration for this man on horseback is qualified by a profound reservation. The spectacle of Fortinbras marching against Poland "to gain a little patch of ground / That hath in it no profit but the name" prompts Hamlet to berate himself for inaction, but he cannot ignore the absurdity of the effort. "Two thousand souls and twenty thousand ducats / Will not debate the question of this straw." The soldiers will risk their very lives "Even for an eggshell" (4.4.19–54). It is only one step from this view of the vanity of ambitious striving to the speculation that great Caesar or Alexander, dead and turned to dust, may one day produce the loam or clay with which to stop the bunghole of a beer barrel. Fortinbras epitomizes the ongoing political order after Hamlet's death, but is that order of any consequence to us after we have imagined with Hamlet the futility of most human endeavor?

To ask such a question is to seek passive or self-abnegating answers to the riddle of life, and Hamlet is attuned to such inquiries. Even before he learns of his father's murder, he contemplates suicide, wishing "that the Everlasting had not fixed / His canon 'gainst self-slaughter" (1.2.131–132). As with the alternative of action, other characters serve as foils to Hamlet, revealing both the attractions and perils of withdrawal. Ophelia is destroyed by meekly acquiescing in others' desires. Whether she commits suicide is uncertain, but the very possibility reminds us that Hamlet has considered and reluctantly rejected this despairing path as forbidden by Christian teaching. He has also playacted at the madness to which Ophelia succumbs. Gertrude identifies herself with Ophelia and, like her, has surrendered her will to male aggressiveness. We suspect she knows little of the actual murder but dares not think how deeply she may be implicated. Her death may possibly be a suicide also, one of atonement. A more attractive alternative to decisive action for Hamlet is acting in the theater, and he is full of advice to the visiting players. The play they perform before Claudius at Hamlet's request and with some lines added by him, a play consciously archaic in style, offers to the Danish court a kind of heightened reflection of itself, a homiletic artifact rendering in conventional terms the taut anxieties and terrors of murder for the sake of ignoble passion. We are not surprised when, in his conversations with the players, Hamlet openly professes his admiration for the way in which art holds "the mirror up to nature, to show virtue her feature, scorn her own image, and the very age and body of the time his form and pressure" (3.2.22–24). Hamlet admires the dramatist's ability to transmute raw human feeling into tragic art, depicting and ordering reality as Shakespeare's play of Hamlet does for us. Yet playacting is also, Hamlet recognizes, a self-indulgent escape for him, a way of unpacking his heart with words, of verbalizing his situation without doing something to remedy it. Acting and talking remind him too much of Polonius, who was an actor in his youth and who continues to be, like Hamlet, an inveterate punster.

Of the passive responses in the play, the stoicism of Horatio is by far the most attractive to Hamlet. "More an antique Roman than a Dane" (5.2.343),

Horatio is, as Hamlet praises him, immune to flattering or to opportunities for cheap self-advancement. He is "As one, in suffering all, that suffers nothing, / A man that Fortune's buffets and rewards / Hast ta'en with equal thanks" (3.2.65–67). Such a person has a sure defense against the worst that life can offer. Hamlet can trust and love Horatio as he can no one else. Yet even here there are limits, for Horatio's skeptical and Roman philosophy cuts him off from a Christian and metaphysical overview. "There are more things in heaven and earth, Horatio, / Than are dreamt of in your philosophy" (1.5.175–176). After they have beheld together the skulls of Yorick's graveyard, Horatio seemingly does not share with Hamlet the exulting Christian perception that, although human life is indeed vain, providence will reveal a pattern transcending human sorrow.

Hamlet's path must lie somewhere between the rash suddenness of Laertes or the canny resoluteness of Fortinbras on the one hand, and the passivity of Ophelia or Gertrude and the stoic resignation of Horatio on the other, but he alternates between action and inaction, finding neither satisfactory. The Ghost has commanded Hamlet to revenge, but has not explained how this is to be done; indeed, Gertrude is to be left passively to heaven and her conscience. If this method will suffice for her (and Christian wisdom taught that such a purgation was as thorough as it was sure), why not for Claudius? If Claudius must be killed, should it be while he is at his sin rather than at his prayers? The play is full of questions, stemming chiefly from the enigmatic commands of the Ghost. "Say, why is this? Wherefore? What should we do?" (1.4.57). Hamlet is not incapable of action. He shows unusual strength and cunning on the pirate ship, or in his duel with Laertes ("I shall win at the odds"; 5.2.209–210), or especially in his slaying of

Polonius—an action hardly characterized by "thinking too precisely on th' event" (4.4.42). Here is forthright action of the sort Laertes espouses. Yet when the corpse behind his mother's arras turns out to be Polonius rather than Claudius, Hamlet knows he has offended heaven. Even if Polonius deserves what he got, Hamlet has made himself into a cruel "scourge" of providence who must himself suffer retribution as well as deal it out. Swift action has not accomplished what the Ghost commanded.

The Ghost in fact does not appear to speak for providence. His message is of revenge, a pagan concept basic to all primitive societies but at odds with Christian teaching. His wish that Claudius be sent to hell and that Gertrude be more gently treated is not the judgment of an impartial deity but the emotional reaction of a murdered man's restless spirit. This is not to say that Hamlet is being tempted to perform a damnable act, as he fears is possible, but that the Ghost's command cannot readily be reconciled with a complex and balanced view of justice. If Hamlet were to spring on Claudius in the fullness of his vice and cut his throat, we would pronounce Hamlet a murderer. What Hamlet believes he has learned instead is that he must become the instrument of providence according to its plans, not his own. After his return from England, he senses triumphantly that all will be for the best if he allows an unseen power to decide the time and place for his final act. Under these conditions, rash action will be right. "Rashly, / And praised be rashness for it—let us know / Our indiscretion sometimes serves us well / When our deep plots do pall, and that should learn us / There's a divinity that shapes our ends, / Rough-hew them how we will" (5.2.6–11). Passivity, too, is now a proper course, for Hamlet puts himself wholly at the disposal of providence. What had seemed so impossible when Hamlet tried to formulate his own design now proves elementary once he trusts to heaven's justice. Rashness and passivity are perfectly fused. Hamlet is revenged without having to commit premeditated murder and is relieved of his painful existence without having to commit suicide.

The circumstances of *Hamlet*'s catastrophe do indeed accomplish all that Hamlet desires, by a route so circuitous that no man could ever have foreseen or devised it. Polonius's death, as it turns out, was instrumental after all, for it led to Laertes's angry return to Denmark and the challenge to a duel. Every seemingly unrelated event has its place; "There is special providence in the fall of a sparrow" (5.2.217–218). Repeatedly the characters stress the role of seeming accident leading to just retribution. Horatio sums up a pattern "Of accidental judgments, casual slaughters . . . And, in this upshot, purposes mistook / Fall'n on th' inventors' heads" (5.2.384–387). Laertes confesses himself "a woodcock to mine own springe" (1.309). As Hamlet had said earlier, of Rosencrantz and Guildenstern, "'tis the sport to have the enginer / Hoist with his own petard" (3.4.213–214). Thus, too, Claudius's poisoned cup, intended for Hamlet, kills the Queen for whom Claudius had done such evil in order to acquire. . . .

[The play's] ending is truly cathartic, for Hamlet dies not as a bloodied avenger but as one who has affirmed the tragic dignity of man. His courage and faith, maintained in the face of great odds, atone for the dismal corruption in which Denmark has festered. His resolutely honest inquiries have taken him beyond the revulsion and doubt that express so eloquently, among other matters, the fearful response of Shakespeare's own generation to a seeming breakdown of established political, theological, and cosmological beliefs. Hamlet finally perceives that "if it be not now, yet it will come," and that "The readiness is all" (5.2.219–220). This discovery, this revelation of necessity and meaning in Hamlet's great reversal of fortune, enables him to confront the tragic circumstance of his life with understanding and heroism, and to demonstrate the triumph of the human spirit even in the moment of his catastrophe.

Such an assertion of the individual will does not lessen the tragic waste with which *Hamlet* ends. Hamlet is dead, the great promise of his life forever lost. Few others have survived. Justice has seemingly been fulfilled in the deaths of Claudius, Gertrude, Rosencrantz and Guildenstern, Polonius, Laertes, and perhaps even Ophelia, but in a wild and extravagant way, as though Justice herself, more vengeful than providential, were unceasingly hungry for victims. Hamlet, the minister of that justice, has likewise grown indifferent to the spilling of blood, even if he submits himself at last to the will of a force he recognizes as providential. Denmark faces the kind of political uncertainty with which the play began. However much Hamlet may admire Fortinbras's resolution, the prince of Norway seems an alien choice for Denmark, even an ironic one. Horatio sees so little point in outliving the catastrophe of this play that he would choose death were it not that he must draw his breath in pain to ensure that Hamlet's story is truly told. Still, that truth has been rescued from oblivion. Amid the ruin of the final scene we share the artist's vision, through which we struggle to interpret and give order to the tragedy of human existence.

Father and Son

by Stanley Kunitz

*The ghost of Hamlet's father is a strange
and horrifying figure, but the reason for
his appearance is not out of the ordinary:
he wants to give his son knowledge and
guidance. In the following poem, the
speaker is a son wanting to hear some
word from his dead father. Stanley Kunitz
mixes the fantastic and the familiar as the
speaker calls back memories and addresses
his father.*

Now in the suburbs and the falling light
I followed him, and now down sandy road
Whiter than bone-dust, through the sweet
Curdle of fields, where the plums
5   Dropped with their load of ripeness, one by one.
Mile after mile I followed, with skimming feet,
After the secret master of my blood,
Him, steeped in the odor of ponds, whose
     indomitable love
Kept me in chains. Strode years; stretched into
     bird;
10 Raced through the sleeping country where I
     was young,
The silence unrolling before me as I came,
The night nailed like an orange to my brow.

How should I tell him my fable and the fears,
How bridge the chasm in a casual tone,
15 Saying, "The house, the stucco one you built,
We lost. Sister married and went from home,

And nothing comes back, it's strange, from
    where she goes.
I lived on a hill that had too many rooms:
Light we could make, but not enough of warmth,
20   And when the light failed, I climbed under
    the hill.
The papers are delivered every day;
I am alone and never shed a tear."

At the water's edge, where the smothering ferns
    lifted
Their arms, "Father!" I cried, "Return! You know
25   The way. I'll wipe the mudstains from your
    clothes;
No trace, I promise, will remain. Instruct
Your son, whirling between two wars,
In the Gemara of your gentleness,
For I would be a child to those who mourn
30   And brother to the foundlings of the field
And friend of innocence and all bright eyes.
O teach me how to work and keep me kind."

Among the turtles and the lilies he turned to me
The white ignorant hollow of his face.

Ophelia

by Arthur Rimbaud
translated by Wallace Fowlie

Of the many tragedies within Hamlet, *one
of the saddest is that of Ophelia, whose
love for Hamlet ends in suffering and
death. This poem by the French poet
Arthur Rimbaud reflects both the beauty
and the tragedy of Ophelia's life.*

I
On the calm black water where the stars sleep
White Ophelia floats like a great lily;
Floats very slowly, lying in her long veils . . .
—You hear in the distant woods sounds of the
    kill.

5   For more than a thousand years sad Ophelia
Has passed, a white phantom, down the long
    black river.
For more than a thousand years her sweet
    madness
Has murmured its romance to the evening breeze.

The wind kisses her breasts and unfolds in a
    wreath
10 Her great veils softly cradled by the waters;
The trembling willows weep on her shoulder,
Over her wide dreaming brow the reeds bend
    down.

The ruffled water lilies sigh around her;
At times she awakens, in a sleeping alder,

15 Some nest, from which escapes a slight rustle of
        wings;
    —A mysterious song falls from the golden stars.

    II
    O pale Ophelia! beautiful as snow!
    Yes, child, you died, carried off by a river!
    —Because the winds falling from the great
        mountains of Norway
20 Had spoken to you in low voices of bitter
        freedom.

    It was a breath, twisting your great hair,
    That bore strange rumors to your dreaming mind;
    It was your heart listening to the song of nature
    In the complaints of the tree and the sighs of
        the nights;

25 It was the voice of mad seas, a great noise,
    That broke your child's heart, too human and
        too soft;
    It was a handsome pale knight, a poor madman
    Who one April morning sat mute at your knees!

    Heaven! Love! Freedom! What a dream, oh
        poor mad girl!
30 You melted to him as snow to a fire;
    Your great visions strangled your words
    —And fearful Infinity terrified your blue eyes!

    III
    —And the Poet says that under the rays of the
        stars
    You come at night to look for the flowers you
        picked,
35 And that he saw on the water, lying in her long
        veils,
    White Ophelia floating, like a great lily.

The Management of Grief

by Bharati Mukherjee

Many of the characters in Hamlet *struggle with grief—Hamlet for his father, Ophelia for Polonius, Laertes for Polonius and Ophelia. In the following story, an Indian woman living in Canada loses her entire family in a plane crash over Ireland. The story portrays the many effects of grief and the intensely personal and individual responses it elicits.*

A woman I don't know is boiling tea the Indian way in my kitchen. There are a lot of women I don't know in my kitchen, whispering, and moving tactfully. They open doors, rummage through the pantry, and try not to ask me where things are kept. They remind me of when my sons were small, on Mother's Day or when Vikram and I were tired, and they would make big, sloppy omelets. I would lie in bed pretending I didn't hear them.

Dr. Sharma, the treasurer of the Indo-Canada Society, pulls me into the hallway. He wants to know if I am worried about money. His wife, who has just come up from the basement with a tray of empty cups and glasses, scolds him. "Don't bother Mrs. Bhave with mundane details." She looks so monstrously pregnant her baby must be days overdue. I tell her she shouldn't be carrying heavy things. "Shaila," she says, smiling, "this is the fifth." Then she grabs a teenager by his shirttails. He slips his Walkman off his head. He has to be one of her four children, they have the same domed and dented foreheads. "What's the official word now?" she demands. The boy slips the headphones back on. "They're acting evasive, Ma. They're saying it could be an accident or a terrorist bomb."

All morning, the boys have been muttering, Sikh Bomb, Sikh Bomb. The men, not using the word, bow their heads in agreement. Mrs. Sharma touches her forehead at such a word. At least they've stopped talking about space debris and Russian lasers.

Two radios are going in the dining room. They are tuned to different stations. Someone must have brought the radios down from my boys' bedrooms. I haven't gone into their rooms since Kusum came running across the front lawn in her bathrobe. She looked so funny, I was laughing when I opened the door.

The big TV in the den is being whizzed through American networks and cable channels.

"Damn!" some man swears bitterly. "How can these preachers carry on like nothing's happened?" I want to tell him we're not that important. You look at the audience, and at the preacher in his blue robe with his beautiful white hair, the potted palm trees under a blue sky, and you know they care about nothing.

The phone rings and rings. Dr. Sharma's taken charge. "We're with her," he keeps saying. "Yes, yes, the doctor has given calming pills. Yes, yes, pills are having necessary effect." I wonder if pills alone explain this calm. Not peace, just a deadening quiet. I was always controlled, but never repressed. Sound can reach me, but my body is tensed, ready to scream. I hear their voices all around me. I hear my boys and Vikram cry, "Mommy, Shaila!" and their screams insulate me, like headphones.

The woman boiling water tells her story again and again. "I got the news first. My cousin called from

Halifax before six a.m., can you imagine? He'd gotten up for prayers and his son was studying for medical exams and he heard on a rock channel that something had happened to a plane. They said first it had disappeared from the radar, like a giant eraser just reached out. His father called me, so I said to him, what do you mean, 'something bad'? You mean a hijacking? And he said, *behn*, there is no confirmation of anything yet, but check with your neighbors because a lot of them must be on that plane. So I called poor Kusum straightaway. I knew Kusum's husband and daughter were booked to go yesterday."

Kusum lives across the street from me. She and Satish had moved in less than a month ago. They said they needed a bigger place. All these people, the Sharmas and friends from the Indo-Canada Society had been there for the housewarming. Satish and Kusum made homemade *tandoori* on their big gas grill and even the white neighbors piled their plates high with that luridly red, charred, juicy chicken. Their younger daughter had danced, and even our boys had broken away from the Stanley Cup telecast to put in a reluctant appearance. Everyone took pictures for their albums and for the community newspapers—another of our families had made it big in Toronto—and now I wonder how many of those happy faces are gone. "Why does God give us so much if all along He intends to take it away?" Kusum asks me.

I nod. We sit on carpeted stairs, holding hands like children. "I never once told him that I loved him," I say. I was too much the well brought up woman. I was so well brought up I never felt comfortable calling my husband by his first name.

"It's all right," Kusum says. "He knew. My husband knew. They felt it. Modern young girls have to say it because what they feel is fake."

Kusum's daughter, Pam, runs in with an overnight case. Pam's in her McDonald's uniform. "Mummy! You have to get dressed!" Panic makes her cranky. "A reporter's on his way here."

"Why?"

"You want to talk to him in your bathrobe?" She starts to brush her mother's long hair. She's the daughter who's always in trouble. She dates Canadian boys and hangs out in the mall, shopping for tight sweaters. The younger one, the goody-goody one according to Pam, the one with a voice so sweet that when she sang *bhajans* for Ethiopian relief even a frugal man like my husband wrote out a hundred dollar check, *she* was on that plane. *She* was going to spend July and August with grandparents because Pam wouldn't go. Pam said she'd rather waitress at McDonald's. "If it's a choice between Bombay and Wonderland, I'm picking Wonderland," she'd said.

"Leave me alone," Kusum yells. "You know what I want to do? If I didn't have to look after you now, I'd hang myself."

Pam's young face goes blotchy with pain. "Thanks," she says, "don't let me stop you."

"Hush," pregnant Mrs. Sharma scolds Pam. "Leave your mother alone. Mr. Sharma will tackle the reporters and fill out the forms. He'll say what has to be said."

Pam stands her ground. "You think I don't know what Mummy's thinking? *Why her?* that's what. That's sick! Mummy wishes my little sister were alive and I were dead."

Kusum's hand in mine is trembly hot. We continue to sit on the stairs.

She calls before she arrives, wondering if there's anything I need. Her name is Judith Templeton and she's an appointee of the provincial government.

"Multiculturalism?" I ask, and she says, "partially," but that her mandate is bigger. "I've been told you knew many of the people on the flight," she says. "Perhaps if you'd agree to help us reach the others . . . ?"

She gives me time at least to put on tea water and pick up the mess in the front room. I have a few *samosas* from Kusum's housewarming that I could fry up, but then I think, why prolong this visit?

Judith Templeton is much younger than she sounded. She wears a blue suit with a white blouse and a polka dot tie. Her blond hair is cut short, her only jewelry is pearl drop earrings. Her briefcase is new and expensive looking, a gleaming cordovan leather. She sits with it across her lap. When she looks out the front windows onto the street, her contact lenses seem to float in front of her light blue eyes.

"What sort of help do you want from me?" I ask. She has refused the tea, out of politeness, but I insist, along with some slightly stale biscuits.

"I have no experience," she admits. "That is, I have an MSW and I've worked in liaison with accident victims, but I mean I have no experience with a tragedy of this scale—"

"Who could?" I ask.

"—and with the complications of culture, language, and customs. Someone mentioned that Mrs. Bhave is a pillar—because you've taken it more calmly."

At this, perhaps, I frown, for she reaches forward, almost to take my hand. "I hope you understand my meaning, Mrs. Bhave. There are hundreds of people in Metro directly affected, like you, and some of them speak no English. There are some widows who've never handled money or gone on a bus, and there are old parents who still haven't eaten or gone outside their bedrooms. Some houses and apartments have been looted. Some wives are still hysterical. Some husbands are in shock and profound depression. We want to help, but our hands are tied in so many ways. We have to distribute money to some people, and there are legal documents—these things can be done. We have interpreters, but we don't always have the human touch, or maybe the right human touch. We don't want to make mistakes, Mrs. Bhave, and that's why we'd like to ask you to help us."

"More mistakes, you mean," I say.

"Police matters are not in my hands," she answers.

"Nothing I can do will make any difference," I say. "We must all grieve in our own way."

"But you are coping very well. All the people said, Mrs. Bhave is the strongest person of all. Perhaps if the others could see you, talk with you, it would help them."

"By the standards of the people you call hysterical, I am behaving very oddly and very badly, Miss Templeton." I want to say to her, *I wish I could scream, starve, walk into Lake Ontario, jump from a bridge.* "They would not see me as a model. I do not see myself as a model."

I am a freak. No one who has ever known me would think of me reacting this way. This terrible calm will not go away.

She asks me if she may call again, after I get back from a long trip that we all must make. "Of course," I say. "Feel free to call, anytime."

Four days later, I find Kusum squatting on a rock overlooking a bay in Ireland. It isn't a big rock, but it juts sharply out over water. This is as close as we'll ever get to them. June breezes balloon out her sari and unpin her knee-length hair. She has the bewildered look of a sea creature whom the tides have stranded.

It's been one hundred hours since Kusum came stumbling and screaming across my lawn. Waiting around the hospital, we've heard many stories. The police, the diplomats, they tell us things thinking that we're strong, that knowledge is helpful to the grieving, and maybe it is. Some, I know, prefer ignorance, or their own versions. The plane broke into two, they say. Unconsciousness was instantaneous. No one suffered. My boys must have just finished their breakfasts. They loved eating on planes, they loved the smallness of plates, knives, and forks. Last year they saved the airline salt and pepper shakers. Half an hour more and they would have made it to Heathrow.

Kusum says that we can't escape our fate. She says that all those people—our husbands, my boys, her girl with the nightingale voice, all those Hindus, Christians, Sikhs, Muslims, Parsis, and atheists on that plane—were fated to die together off this beautiful bay. She learned this from a swami in Toronto.

I have my Valium.

Six of us "relatives"—two widows and four widowers—choose to spend the day today by the waters instead of sitting in a hospital room and scanning photographs of the dead. That's what they call us now: relatives. I've looked through twenty-seven photos in two days. They're very kind to us, the Irish are very understanding. Sometimes understanding means freeing a tourist bus for this trip to the bay, so we can pretend to spy our loved ones through the glassiness of waves or in sun-speckled cloud shapes.

I could die here, too, and be content.

"What is that, out there?" She's standing and flapping her hands and for a moment I see a head shape bobbing in the waves. She's standing in the water, I, on the boulder. The tide is low, and a round, black, head-sized rock has just risen from the waves. She returns, her sari end dripping and ruined and her face is a twisted remnant of hope, the way mine was a hundred hours ago, still laughing but inwardly knowing that nothing but the ultimate tragedy could bring two women together at six o'clock on a Sunday morning. I watch her face sag into blankness.

"That water felt warm, Shaila," she says at length.

"You can't," I say. "We have to wait for our turn to come."

I haven't eaten in four days, haven't brushed my teeth.

"I know," she says. "I tell myself I have no right to grieve. They are in a better place than we are. My swami says I should be thrilled for them. My swami says depression is a sign of our selfishness."

Maybe I'm selfish. Selfishly I break away from Kusum and run, sandals slapping against stones, to the water's edge. What if my boys aren't lying pinned under the debris? What if they aren't stuck a mile below that innocent blue chop? What if, given the strong currents . . .

Now I've ruined my sari, one of my best. Kusum has joined me, knee-deep in water that feels to me like a swimming pool. I could settle in the water, and my husband would take my hand and the boys would slap water in my face just to see me scream.

"Do you remember what good swimmers my boys were, Kusum?"

"I saw the medals," she says.

One of the widowers, Dr. Ranganathan from Montreal, walks out to us, carrying his shoes in one hand. He's an electrical engineer. Someone at the hotel mentioned his work is famous around the world, something about the place where physics and electricity come together. He has lost a huge family, something indescribable. "With some luck," Dr. Ranganathan suggests to me, "a good swimmer could make it safely to some island. It is quite possible that there may be many, many microscopic islets scattered around."

"You're not just saying that?" I tell Dr. Ranganathan about Vinod, my elder son. Last year he took diving as well.

"It's a parent's duty to hope," he says. "It is foolish to rule out possibilities that have not been tested. I myself have not surrendered hope."

Kusum is sobbing once again. "Dear lady," he says, laying his free hand on her arm, and she calms down.

"Vinod is how old?" he asks me. He's very careful, as we all are. *Is*, not was.

"Fourteen. Yesterday he was fourteen. His father and uncle were going to take him down to the Taj and give him a big birthday party. I couldn't go with them because I couldn't get two weeks off from my stupid job in June." I process bills for a travel agent. June is a big travel month.

Dr. Ranganathan whips the pockets of his suit jacket inside out. Squashed roses, in darkening shades of pink, float on the water. He tore the roses off creepers in somebody's garden. He didn't ask anyone if he could pluck the roses, but now there's been an article about it in the local papers. When you see an Indian person, it says, please give him or her flowers.

"A strong youth of fourteen," he says, "can very likely pull to safety a younger one."

My sons, though four years apart, were very close. Vinod wouldn't let Mithun drown. *Electrical engineering*, I think, foolishly perhaps: this man knows important secrets of the universe, things closed to me. Relief spins me lightheaded. No wonder my boys' photographs haven't turned up in the gallery of photos of the recovered dead. "Such pretty roses," I say.

"My wife loved pink roses. Every Friday I had to bring a bunch home. I used to say, why? After twenty odd years of marriage you're still needing proof positive of my love?" He has identified his wife and three of his children. Then others from Montreal, the lucky ones, intact families with no survivors. He chuckles as he wades back to shore. Then he swings around to ask me a question. "Mrs. Bhave, you are wanting to throw in some roses for your loved ones? I have two big ones left."

But I have other things to float: Vinod's pocket calculator; a half-painted model B-52 for my Mithun. They'd want them on their island. And for my husband? For him I let fall into the calm, glassy waters a poem I wrote in the hospital yesterday. Finally he'll know my feelings for him.

"Don't tumble, the rocks are slippery," Dr. Ranganathan cautions. He holds out a hand for me to grab.

Then it's time to get back on the bus, time to rush back to our waiting posts on hospital benches.

Kusum is one of the lucky ones. The lucky ones flew here, identified in multiplicate their loved ones, then will fly to India with the bodies for proper ceremonies. Satish is one of the few males who surfaced. The photos of faces we saw on the walls in an office at Heathrow and here in the hospital are mostly of women. Women have more body fat, a nun said to me matter-of-factly. They float better.

Today I was stopped by a young sailor on the street. He had loaded bodies, he'd gone into the water when—he checks my face for signs of strength—when the sharks were first spotted. I don't blush, and he breaks down. "It's all right," I say. "Thank you." I had heard about the sharks from Dr. Ranganathan. In his orderly mind, science brings understanding, it holds no terror. It is the shark's duty. For every deer there is a hunter, for every fish a fisherman.

The Irish are not shy; they rush to me and give me hugs and some are crying. I cannot imagine reactions like that on the streets of Toronto. Just strangers, and I am touched. Some carry flowers with them and give them to any Indian they see.

After lunch, a policeman I have gotten to know quite well catches hold of me. He says he thinks he has a match for Vinod. I explain what a good swimmer Vinod is.

"You want me with you when you look at photos?" Dr. Ranganathan walks ahead of me into the picture gallery. In these matters, he is a scientist, and I am grateful. It is a new perspective. "They have performed miracles," he says. "We are indebted to them."

The first day or two the policemen showed us relatives only one picture at a time; now they're in a hurry, they're eager to lay out the possibles, and even the probables.

The face on the photo is of a boy much like Vinod; the same intelligent eyes, the same thick brows dipping into a V. But this boy's features, even his cheeks, are puffier, wider, mushier.

"No." My gaze is pulled by other pictures. There are five other boys who look like Vinod.

The nun assigned to console me rubs the first picture with a fingertip. "When they've been in the water for a while, love, they look a little heavier." The bones under the skin are broken, they said on the first day—try to adjust your memories. It's important.

"It's not him. I'm his mother. I'd know."

"I know this one!" Dr. Ranganathan cries out suddenly from the back of the gallery. "And this one!" I think he senses that I don't want to find my boys. "They are the Kutty brothers. They were also from Montreal." I don't mean to be crying. On the contrary, I am ecstatic. My suitcase in the hotel is packed heavy with dry clothes for my boys.

The policeman starts to cry. "I am so sorry, I am so sorry, ma'am. I really thought we had a match."

With the nun ahead of us and the policeman behind, we, the unlucky ones without our children's bodies, file out of the makeshift gallery.

From Ireland most of us go on to India. Kusum and I take the same direct flight to Bombay, so I can help her clear customs quickly. But we have to argue with a man in uniform. He has large boils on his face. The boils swell and glow with sweat as we argue with him. He wants Kusum to wait in line and he refuses to take authority because his boss is on a tea break. But Kusum won't let her coffins out of sight, and I shan't desert her though I know that my parents, elderly and diabetic, must be waiting in a stuffy car in a scorching lot.

"You bastard!" I scream at the man with the popping boils. Other passengers press closer. "You think we're smuggling contraband in those coffins!"

Once upon a time we were well brought up women; we were dutiful wives who kept our heads veiled, our voices shy and sweet.

In India, I become, once again, an only child of rich, ailing parents. Old friends of the family come to pay their respects. Some are Sikh, and inwardly, involuntarily, I cringe. My parents are progressive people; they do not blame communities for a few individuals.

In Canada it is a different story now.

"Stay longer," my mother pleads. "Canada is a cold place. Why would you want to be all by yourself?" I stay.

Three months pass. Then another.

"Vikram wouldn't have wanted you to give up things!" they protest. They call my husband by the name he was born with. In Toronto he'd changed to Vik so the men he worked with at his office would find his name as easy as Rod or Chris. "You know, the dead aren't cut off from us!"

My grandmother, the spoiled daughter of a rich *zamindar*, shaved her head with rusty razor blades when she was widowed at sixteen. My grandfather died of childhood diabetes when he was nineteen, and she saw herself as the harbinger of bad luck. My mother grew up without parents, raised indifferently by an uncle, while her true mother slept in a hut behind the main estate house and took her food with the servants. She grew up a rationalist. My parents abhor mindless mortification.

The zamindar's daughter kept stubborn faith in Vedic rituals; my parents rebelled. I am trapped between two modes of knowledge. At thirty-six, I am too old to start over and too young to give up. Like my husband's spirit, I flutter between worlds.

Courting aphasia, we travel. We travel with our phalanx of servants and poor relatives. To hill stations and to beach resorts. We play contract bridge in dusty gymkhana clubs. We ride stubby ponies up crumbly mountain trails. At tea dances, we let ourselves be twirled twice round the ballroom. We hit the holy spots we hadn't made time for before. In Varanasi, Kalighat, Rishikesh, Hardwar, astrologers and palmists seek me out and for a fee offer me cosmic consolations.

Already the widowers among us are being shown new bride candidates. They cannot resist the call of custom, the authority of their parents and older brothers. They must marry; it is the duty of a man to look after a wife. The new wives will be young widows with children, destitute but of good family. They will make loving wives, but the men will shun them. I've had calls from the men over crackling Indian telephone lines. "Save me," they say, these substantial, educated, successful men of forty. "My parents are arranging a marriage for me." In a month they will have buried one family and returned to Canada with a new bride and partial family.

I am comparatively lucky. No one here thinks of arranging a husband for an unlucky widow.

Then, on the third day of the sixth month into this odyssey, in an abandoned temple in a tiny Himalayan village, as I make my offering of flowers and sweetmeats to the god of a tribe of animists, my husband descends to me. He is squatting next to a scrawny *sadhu* in moth-eaten robes. Vikram wears the vanilla suit he wore the last time I hugged him. The *sadhu* tosses petals on a butter-fed flame, reciting Sanskrit mantras and sweeps his face of flies. My husband takes my hands in his.

You're beautiful, he starts. Then, *What are you doing here?*

Shall I stay? I ask. He only smiles, but already the image is fading. *You must finish alone what we started together*. No seaweed wreathes his mouth. He speaks too fast just as he used to when we were an envied family in our pink split-level. He is gone.

In the windowless altar room, smoky with joss sticks and clarified butter lamps, a sweaty hand gropes for my blouse. I do not shriek. The *sadhu* arranges his robe. The lamps hiss and sputter out.

When we come out of the temple, my mother says, "Did you feel something weird in there?"

My mother has no patience with ghosts, prophetic dreams, holy men, and cults.

"No," I lie. "Nothing."

But she knows that she's lost me. She knows that in days I shall be leaving.

Kusum's put her house up for sale. She wants to live in an ashram in Hardwar. Moving to Hardwar was her swami's idea. Her swami runs two ashrams, the one in Hardwar and another here in Toronto.

"Don't run away," I tell her.

"I'm not running away," she says. "I'm pursuing inner peace. You think you or that Ranganathan fellow are better off?"

Pam's left for California. She wants to do some modelling, she says. She says when she comes into her share of the insurance money she'll open a yoga-cum-aerobics studio in Hollywood. She sends me postcards so naughty I daren't leave them on the coffee table. Her mother has withdrawn from her and the world.

The rest of us don't lose touch, that's the point. Talk is all we have, says Dr. Ranganathan, who has also resisted his relatives and returned to Montreal and to his job, alone. He says, whom better to talk with than other relatives? We've been melted down and recast as a new tribe.

He calls me twice a week from Montreal. Every Wednesday night and every Saturday afternoon. He is changing jobs, going to Ottawa. But Ottawa is over a hundred miles away, and he is forced to drive two hundred and twenty miles a day. He can't bring himself to sell his house. The house is a temple, he says; the king-sized bed in the master bedroom is a shrine. He sleeps on a folding cot. A devotee.

There are still some hysterical relatives. Judith Templeton's list of those needing help and those who've "accepted" is in nearly perfect balance. Acceptance means you speak of your family in the past tense and you make active plans for moving ahead with your life. There are courses at Seneca and Ryerson we could be taking. Her gleaming leather briefcase is full of college catalogues and lists of cultural societies that need our help. She has done impressive work, I tell her.

"In the textbooks on grief management," she replies—I am her confidante, I realize, one of the few whose grief has not sprung bizarre obsessions—"there are stages to pass through: rejection, depression, acceptance, reconstruction." She has compiled a chart and finds that six months after the tragedy, none of us still reject reality, but only a handful are reconstructing. "Depressed Acceptance" is the plateau we've reached. Remarriage is a major step in reconstruction (though she's a little surprised, even shocked, over *how* quickly some of the men have taken on new families). Selling one's house and changing jobs and cities is healthy.

How do I tell Judith Templeton that my family surrounds me, and that like creatures in epics, they've changed shapes? She sees me as calm and accepting but worries that I have no job, no career. My closest friends are worse off than I. I cannot tell her my days, even my nights, are thrilling.

She asks me to help with families she can't reach at all. An elderly couple in Agincourt whose sons were killed just weeks after they had brought their parents over from a village in Punjab. From their names, I know they are Sikh. Judith Templeton and a translator have visited them twice with offers of money for air fare to Ireland, with bank forms, power-of-attorney forms, but they have refused to sign, or to leave their tiny apartment. Their sons' money is frozen in the bank. Their sons' investment apartments have been trashed by tenants, the furnishings sold off. The parents fear that anything they sign or any money they receive will end the company's or the country's obligations to them. They fear they are selling their sons for two airline tickets to a place they've never seen.

The high-rise apartment is a tower of Indians and West Indians, with a sprinkling of Orientals. The nearest bus stop kiosk is lined with women in saris. Boys practice cricket in the parking lot. Inside the building, even I wince a bit from the ferocity of onion fumes, the distinctive and immediate Indianness of frying *ghee*, but Judith Templeton maintains a steady flow of information. These poor old people are in imminent danger of losing their place and all their services.

I say to her, "They are Sikh. They will not open up to a Hindu woman." And what I want to add is, as much as I try not to, I stiffen now at the sight of beards and turbans. I remember a time when we all trusted each other in this new country, it was only the new country we worried about.

The two rooms are dark and stuffy. The lights are off, and an oil lamp sputters on the coffee table. The bent old lady has let us in, and her husband is wrapping a white turban over his oiled, hip-length hair. She immediately goes to the kitchen, and I hear the most familiar sound of an Indian home, tap water hitting and filling a teapot.

They have not paid their utility bills, out of fear and the inability to write a check. The telephone is gone; electricity and gas and water are soon to follow. They have told Judith their sons will provide. They are good boys, and they have always earned and looked after their parents.

We converse a bit in Hindi. They do not ask about the crash and I wonder if I should bring it up. If they think I am here merely as a translator, then they may feel insulted. There are thousands of Punjabi-speakers, Sikhs, in Toronto to do a better job. And so I say to the old lady, "I too have lost my sons, and my husband, in the crash."

Her eyes immediately fill with tears. The man

mutters a few words which sound like a blessing. "God provides and God takes away," he says.

I want to say, but only men destroy and give back nothing. "My boys and my husband are not coming back," I say. "We have to understand that."

Now the old woman responds. "But who is to say? Man alone does not decide these things." To this her husband adds his agreement.

Judith asks about the bank papers, the release forms. With a stroke of the pen, they will have a provincial trustee to pay their bills, invest their money, send them a monthly pension.

"Do you know this woman?" I ask them.

The man raises his hand from the table, turns it over and seems to regard each finger separately before he answers. "This young lady is always coming here, we make tea for her and she leaves papers for us to sign." His eyes scan a pile of papers in the corner of the room. "Soon we will be out of tea, then will she go away?"

The old lady adds, "I have asked my neighbors and no one else gets *angrezi* visitors. What have we done?"

"It's her job," I try to explain. "The government is worried. Soon you will have no place to stay, no lights, no gas, no water."

"Government will get its money. Tell her not to worry, we are honorable people."

I try to explain the government wishes to give money, not take. He raises his hand. "Let them take," he says. "We are accustomed to that. That is no problem."

"We are strong people," says the wife. "Tell her that."

"Who needs all this machinery?" demands the husband. "It is unhealthy, the bright lights, the cold air on a hot day, the cold food, the four gas rings. God will provide, not government."

"When our boys return," the mother says. Her husband sucks his teeth. "Enough talk," he says.

Judith breaks in. "Have you convinced them?" The snaps on her cordovan briefcase go off like firecrackers in that quiet apartment. She lays the sheaf of legal papers on the coffee table. "If they can't write their names, an X will do—I've told them that."

Now the old lady has shuffled to the kitchen and soon emerges with a pot of tea and two cups. "I think my bladder will go first on a job like this," Judith says to me, smiling. "If only there was some way of reaching them. Please thank her for the tea. Tell her she's very kind."

I nod in Judith's direction and tell them in Hindi, "She thanks you for the tea. She thinks you are being very hospitable but she doesn't have the slightest idea what it means."

I want to say, humor her. I want to say, my boys and my husband are with me too, more than ever. I look in the old man's eyes and I can read his stubborn, peasant's message: *I have protected this woman as best I can. She is the only person I have left. Give to me or take from me what you will, but I will not sign for it. I will not pretend that I accept.*

In the car, Judith says, "You see what I'm up against? I'm sure they're lovely people, but their stubbornness and ignorance are driving me crazy. They think signing a paper is signing their sons' death warrants, don't they?"

I am looking out the window. I want to say, *In our culture, it is a parent's duty to hope.*

"Now Shaila, this next woman is a real mess. She cries day and night, and she refuses all medical help. We may have to—"

"—Let me out at the subway," I say.

"I beg your pardon?" I can feel those blue eyes staring at me.

It would not be like her to disobey. She merely disapproves, and slows at a corner to let me out. Her voice is plaintive. "Is there anything I said? Anything I did?"

I could answer her suddenly in a dozen ways, but I choose not to. "Shaila? Let's talk about it," I hear, then slam the door.

A wife and mother begins her new life in a new country, and that life is cut short. Yet her husband tells her: Complete what we have started. We, who stayed out of politics and came halfway around the world to avoid religious and political feuding, have been the first in the New World to die from it. I no longer know what we started, nor how to complete it. I write letters to the editors of local papers and to members of Parliament. Now at least they admit it was a bomb. One MP answers back, with sympathy, but with a challenge. You want to make a difference? Work on a campaign. Work on mine. Politicize the Indian voter.

My husband's old lawyer helps me set up a trust. Vikram was a saver and a careful investor. He had saved the boys' boarding school and college fees. I sell the pink house at four times what we paid for it and take a small apartment downtown. I am looking for a charity to support.

We are deep in the Toronto winter, gray skies, icy pavements. I stay indoors, watching television. I have tried to assess my situation, how best to live my life, to complete what we began so many years ago. Kusum has written me from Hardwar that her life is now serene. She has seen Satish and has heard her daughter sing again. Kusum was on a pilgrimage, passing through a village when she heard a young girl's voice, singing one of her daughter's favorite *bhajans*. She followed the music through the squalor of a

Himalayan village, to a hut where a young girl, an exact replica of her daughter, was fanning coals under the kitchen fire. When she appeared, the girl cried out, "Ma!" and ran away. What did I think of that?

I think I can only envy her.

Pam didn't make it to California, but writes me from Vancouver. She works in a department store, giving make-up hints to Indian and Oriental girls. Dr. Ranganathan has given up his commute, given up his house and job, and accepted an academic position in Texas where no one knows his story and he has vowed not to tell it. He calls me now once a week.

I wait, I listen, and I pray, but Vikram has not returned to me. The voices and the shapes and the nights filled with visions ended abruptly several weeks ago.

I take it as a sign.

One rare, beautiful, sunny day last week, returning from a small errand on Yonge Street, I was walking through the park from the subway to my apartment. I live equidistant from the Ontario Houses of Parliament and the University of Toronto. The day was not cold, but something in the bare trees caught my attention. I looked up from the gravel, into the branches and the clear blue sky beyond. I thought I heard the rustling of larger forms, and I waited a moment for voices. Nothing.

"What?" I asked.

Then as I stood in the path looking north to Queen's Park and west to the university, I heard the voices of my family one last time. *Your time has come*, they said. *Go, be brave.*

I do not know where this voyage I have begun will end. I do not know which direction I will take. I dropped the package on a park bench and started walking.

Tell Them Not to Kill Me!

by Juan Rulfo
translated by George D. Schade

*Revenge for the death of his father is a
central motive for Hamlet and a powerful
force in the play. In this story, Juan Rulfo
explores in a different time and place the
avenging of a murder.*

"Tell them not to kill me, Justino! Go on and tell
them that. For God's sake! Tell them. Tell them please
for God's sake."

"I can't. There's a sergeant there who doesn't want
to hear anything about you."

"Make him listen to you. Use your wits and tell him
that scaring me has been enough. Tell him please for
God's sake."

"But it's not just to scare you. It seems they really
mean to kill you. And I don't want to go back there."

"Go on once more. Just once, to see what you can
do."

"No. I don't feel like going. Because if I do they'll
know I'm your son. If I keep bothering them they'll
end up knowing who I am and will decide to shoot me
too. Better leave things the way they are now."

"Go on, Justino. Tell them to take a little pity on
me. Just tell them that."

Justino clenched his teeth and shook his head
saying no.

And he kept on shaking his head for some time.

"Tell the sergeant to let you see the colonel. And tell

him how old I am— How little I'm worth. What will he get out of killing me? Nothing. After all he must have a soul. Tell him to do it for the blessed salvation of his soul."

Justino got up from the pile of stones which he was sitting on and walked to the gate of the corral. Then he turned around to say, "All right, I'll go. But if they decide to shoot me too, who'll take care of my wife and kids?"

"Providence will take care of them, Justino. You go there now and see what you can do for me. That's what matters."

They'd brought him in at dawn. The morning was well along now and he was still there, tied to a post, waiting. He couldn't keep still. He'd tried to sleep for a while to calm down, but he couldn't. He wasn't hungry either. All he wanted was to live. Now that he knew they were really going to kill him, all he could feel was his great desire to stay alive, like a recently resuscitated man.

Who would've thought that old business that happened so long ago and that was buried the way he thought it was would turn up? That business when he had to kill Don Lupe. Not for nothing either, as the Alimas tried to make out, but because he had his reasons. He remembered: Don Lupe Terreros, the owner of the Puerta de Piedra—and besides that, his compadre—was the one he, Juvencio Nava, had to kill, because he'd refused to let him pasture his animals, when he was the owner of the Puerta de Piedra and his compadre too.

At first he didn't do anything because he felt compromised. But later, when the drought came, when he saw how his animals were dying off one by one, plagued by hunger, and how his compadre Lupe continued to refuse to let him use his pastures, then was when he began breaking through the fence and driving his herd of skinny animals to the pasture where they could get their fill of grass. And Don Lupe didn't like it and ordered the fence mended, so that he, Juvencio Nava, had to cut open the hole again. So, during the day the hole was stopped up and at night it was opened again, while the stock stayed there right next to the fence, always waiting—his stock that before had lived just smelling the grass without being able to taste it.

And he and Don Lupe argued again and again without coming to any agreement.

Until one day Don Lupe said to him, "Look here, Juvencio, if you let another animal in my pasture, I'll kill it."

And he answered him, "Look here, Don Lupe, it's not my fault that the animals look out for themselves. They're innocent. You'll have to pay for it, if you kill them."

And he killed one of my yearlings.

This happened thirty-five years ago in March, because in April I was already up in the mountains, running away from the summons. The ten cows I gave the judge didn't do me any good, or the lien on my house either, to pay for getting me out of jail. Still later they used up what was left to pay so they wouldn't keep after me, but they kept after me just the same. That's why I came to live with my son on this other piece of land of mine which is called Palo de Venado. And my son grew up and got married to my daughter-in-law Ignacia and has had eight children now. So it happened a long time ago and ought to be forgotten by now. But I guess it's not.

I figured then that with about a hundred pesos everything could be fixed up. The dead Don Lupe left just his wife and two little kids still crawling. And his widow died soon afterward too—they say from grief.

They took the kids far off to some relatives. So there was nothing to fear from them.

But the rest of the people took the position that I was still summoned to be tried just to scare me so they could keep on robbing me. Every time someone came to the village they told me, "There are some strangers in town, Juvencio."

And I would take off to the mountains, hiding among the madrone thickets and passing the days with nothing to eat but herbs. Sometimes I had to go out at midnight, as though the dogs were after me. It's been that way my whole life. Not just a year or two. My whole life.

And now they'd come for him when he no longer expected anyone, confident that people had forgotten all about it, believing that he'd spend at least his last days peacefully. "At least," he thought, "I'll have some peace in my old age. They'll leave me alone."

He'd clung to this hope with all his heart. That's why it was hard for him to imagine that he'd die like this, suddenly, at this time of life, after having fought so much to ward off death, after having spent his best years running from one place to another because of the alarms, now when his body had become all dried up and leathery from the bad days when he had to be in hiding from everybody.

Hadn't he even let his wife go off and leave him? The day when he learned his wife had left him, the idea of going out in search of her didn't even cross his mind. He let her go without trying to find out at all who she went with or where, so he wouldn't have to go down to the village. He let her go as he'd let everything else go, without putting up a fight. All he had left to take care of was his life, and he'd do that, if nothing else. He couldn't let them kill him. He couldn't. Much less now.

But that's why they brought him from there, from

Palo de Venado. They didn't need to tie him so he'd follow them. He walked alone, tied by his fear. They realized he couldn't run with his old body, with those skinny legs of his like dry bark, cramped up with the fear of dying. Because that's where he was headed. For death. They told him so.

That's when he knew. He began to feel that stinging in his stomach that always came on suddenly when he saw death nearby, making his eyes big with fear and his mouth swell up with those mouthfuls of sour water he had to swallow unwillingly. And that thing that made his feet heavy while his head felt soft and his heart pounded with all its force against his ribs. No, he couldn't get used to the idea that they were going to kill him.

There must be some hope. Somewhere there must still be some hope left. Maybe they'd made a mistake. Perhaps they were looking for another Juvencio Nava and not him.

He walked along in silence between those men, with his arms fallen at his sides. The early-morning hour was dark, starless. The wind blew slowly, whipping the dry earth back and forth, which was filled with that odor like urine that dusty roads have.

His eyes, that had become squinty with the years, were looking down at the ground, here under his feet, in spite of the darkness. There in the earth was his whole life. Sixty years of living on it, of holding it tight in his hands, of tasting it like one tastes the flavor of meat. For a long time he'd been crumbling it with his eyes, savoring each piece as if it were the last one, almost knowing it would be the last.

Then, as if wanting to say something, he looked at the men who were marching along next to him. He was going to tell them to let him loose, to let him go; "I haven't hurt anybody, boys," he was going to say to them, but he kept silent. "A little further on I'll tell them," he thought. And he just looked at them. He could even imagine they were his friends, but he didn't want to. They weren't. He didn't know who they were. He watched them moving at his side and bending down from time to time to see where the road continued.

He'd seen them for the first time at nightfall, that dusky hour when everything seems scorched. They'd crossed the furrows trodding on the tender corn. And he'd gone down on account of that—to tell them that the corn was beginning to grow there. But that didn't stop them.

He'd seen them in time. He'd always had the luck to see everything in time. He could've hidden, gone up in the mountains for a few hours until they left and then come down again. Already it was time for the rains to have come, but the rains didn't come and the corn was beginning to wither. Soon it'd be all dried up.

So it hadn't even been worthwhile, his coming down and placing himself among those men like in a hole, never to get out again.

And now he continued beside them, holding back how he wanted to tell them to let him go. He didn't see their faces, he only saw their bodies, which swung toward him and then away from him. So when he started talking he didn't know if they'd heard him. He said, "I've never hurt anybody." That's what he said. But nothing changed. Not one of the bodies seemed to pay attention. The faces didn't turn to look at him. They kept right on, as if they were walking in their sleep.

Then he thought that there was nothing else he could say, that he would have to look for hope somewhere else. He let his arms fall again to his sides and went by the first houses of the village, among those four men, darkened by the black color of the night.

"Colonel, here is the man."

They'd stopped in front of the narrow doorway. He stood with his hat in his hand, respectfully, waiting to see someone come out. But only the voice came out, "Which man?"

"From Palo de Venado, colonel. The one you ordered us to bring in."

"Ask him if he ever lived in Alima," came the voice from inside again.

"Hey, you. Ever lived in Alima?" the sergeant facing him repeated the question.

"Yes. Tell the colonel that's where I'm from. And that I lived there till not long ago."

"Ask him if he knew Guadalupe Terreros."

"He says did you know Guadalupe Terreros?"

"Don Lupe? Yes. Tell him that I knew him. He's dead."

Then the voice inside changed tone: "I know he died," it said. And the voice continued talking, as if it was conversing with someone there on the other side of the reed wall.

"Guadalupe Terreros was my father. When I grew up and looked for him they told me he was dead. It's hard to grow up knowing that the thing we have to hang on to to take roots from is dead. That's what happened to us.

"Later on I learned that he was killed by being hacked first with a machete and then an ox goad stuck in his belly. They told me he lasted more than two days and that when they found him, lying in an arroyo, he was still in agony and begging that his family be taken care of.

"As time goes by you seem to forget this. You try to forget it. What you can't forget is finding out that the one who did it is still alive, feeding his rotten soul with the illusion of eternal life. I couldn't forgive that man, even though I don't know him; but the fact that I know where he is makes me want to finish him off. I can't forgive his still living. He should never have been born."

From here, from outside, all he said was clearly heard. Then he ordered, "Take him and tie him up awhile, so he'll suffer, and then shoot him!"

"Look at me, colonel!" he begged. "I'm not worth anything now. It won't be long before I die all by myself, crippled by old age. Don't kill me!"

"Take him away!" repeated the voice from inside.

"I've already paid, colonel. I've paid many times over. They took everything away from me. They punished me in many ways. I've spent about forty years hiding like a leper, always with the fear they'd kill me at any moment. I don't deserve to die like this, colonel. Let the Lord pardon me, at least. Don't kill me! Tell them not to kill me!"

There he was, as if they'd beaten him, waving his hat against the ground. Shouting.

Immediately the voice from inside said, "Tie him up and give him something to drink until he gets drunk so the shots won't hurt him."

Finally, now, he'd been quieted. There he was, slumped down at the foot of the post. His son Justino had come and his son Justino had gone and had returned and now was coming again.

He slung him on top of the burro. He cinched him up tight against the saddle so he wouldn't fall off on the road. He put his head in a sack so it wouldn't give such a bad impression. And then he made the burro giddap, and away they went in a hurry to reach Palo de Venado in time to arrange the wake for the dead man.

"Your daughter-in-law and grandchildren will miss you," he was saying to him. "They'll look at your face and won't believe it's you. They'll think the coyote has been eating on you when they see your face full of holes from all those bullets they shot at you."

Hamlet

by Yevgeny Vinokurov
translated by Daniel Weissbort

*The character of Hamlet has been played
by many actors, and the play has
fascinated audiences in many countries,
including Russia. In this poem, the staging
of the tragedy in a Russian military camp
puts Hamlet in a new light.*

We rigged up a theater behind the storehouse
With posts and cross beams.
Lance Corporal Dyadin played Hamlet
And raised his arms in anguish.
5   The CO, I remember, always said
Of him he was a good man.
He was stolid, red-cheeked, thickset,
And his face was a mass of freckles.
When he came on, he'd hang his head,
10   Folding his arms mournfully, but
Somehow, as soon as he said
"To be or not to be?" everyone laughed.
I have seen many Hamlets stepping out
Of the dark wings into the spotlight,
15   Tragic, with booming voices, spindle-legged.
At the first word, a hush descends,
Hearts stop beating, opera glasses tremble.
These Hamlets have passion, power, art!
But ours froze and shivered in the damp with us
20   And shared our fire's warmth.

Japanese Hamlet

by Toshio Mori

Many characters in Hamlet are driven by powerful and complicated emotions. In this story, a young man's desire to become a Shakespearean actor and play the part of Hamlet takes on a driving force of its own.

He used to come to the house and ask me to hear him recite. Each time he handed me a volume of *The Complete Works of William Shakespeare*. He never forgot to do that. He wanted me to sit in front of him, open the book, and follow him as he recited his lines. I did willingly. There was little for me to do in the evenings so when Tom Fukunaga came over I was ready to help out almost any time. And as his love for Shakespeare's plays grew with the years he did not want anything else in the world but to be a Shakespearean actor.

Tom Fukunaga was a schoolboy in a Piedmont home. He had been one since his freshman days in high school. When he was thirty-one he was still a schoolboy. Nobody knew his age but he and the relatives. Every time his relatives came to the city they put up a roar and said he was a good-for-nothing loafer and ought to be ashamed of himself for being a schoolboy at this age.

"I am not loafing," he told his relatives. "I am studying very hard."

One of his uncles came often to the city to see him. He tried a number of times to persuade Tom to quit stage hopes and schoolboy attitude. "Your parents have already disowned you. Come to your senses," he said. "You should go out and earn a man's salary. You are alone now. Pretty soon even your relatives will drop you."

"That's all right," Tom Fukunaga said. He kept shaking his head until his uncle went away.

When Tom Fukunaga came over to the house he used to tell me about his parents and relatives in the country. He told me in particular about the uncle who kept coming back to warn and persuade him. Tom said he really was sorry for Uncle Bill to take the trouble to see him.

"Why don't you work for someone in the daytime and study at night?" I said to Tom.

"I cannot be bothered with such a change at this time," he said. "Besides, I get five dollars a week plus room and board. That is enough for me. If I should go out and work for someone I would have to pay for room and board besides carfare so I would not be richer. And even if I should save a little more it would not help me become a better Shakespearean actor."

When we came down to the business of recitation there was no recess. Tom Fukunaga wanted none of it. He would place a cup of water before him and never touch it. "Tonight we'll begin with Hamlet," he said many times during the years. *Hamlet* was his favorite play. When he talked about Shakespeare to anyone he began by mentioning Hamlet. He played parts in other plays but always he came back to Hamlet: This was his special role, the role which would establish him in Shakespearean history.

There were moments when I was afraid that Tom's energy and time were wasted and I helped along to waste it. We were miles away from the stage world. Tom Fukunaga had not seen a backstage. He was just as far from the stagedoor in his thirties as he was in his high school days. Sometimes as I sat holding

Shakespeare's book and listening to Tom I must have looked worried and discouraged.

"Come on, come on!" he said. "Have you got the blues?"

One day I told him the truth: I was afraid we were not getting anywhere, that perhaps we were attempting the impossible. "If you could contact the stage people it might help," I said. "Otherwise we are wasting our lives."

"I don't think so," Tom said. "I am improving every day. That is what counts. Our time will come later."

That night we took up *Macbeth*. He went through his parts smoothly. This made him feel good. "Some day I'll be the ranking Shakespearean actor," he said.

Sometimes I told him I liked best to hear him recite the sonnets. I thought he was better with the sonnets than in the parts of Macbeth or Hamlet.

"I'd much rather hear you recite his sonnets, Tom," I said.

"Perhaps you like his sonnets best of all," he said. "Hamlet is my forte. I know I am at my best playing Hamlet."

For a year Tom Fukunaga did not miss a week coming to the house. Each time he brought a copy of Shakespeare's complete works and asked me to hear him say the lines. For better or worse he was not a bit downhearted. He still had no contact with the stage people. He did not talk about his uncle who kept coming back urging him to quit. I found out later that his uncle did not come to see him any more.

In the meantime Tom stayed at the Piedmont home as a schoolboy. He accepted his five dollars a week just as he had done years ago when he was a freshman at Piedmont High. This fact did not bother Tom at all when I mentioned it to him. "What are you worrying for?" he said. "I know I am taking chances. I went into this with my eyes open so don't worry."

But I could not get over worrying about Tom Fukunaga's chances. Every time he came over I felt bad for he was wasting his life and for the fact that I was mixed in it. Several times I told him to go somewhere and find a job. He laughed. He kept coming to the house and asked me to sit and hear him recite Hamlet.

The longer I came to know Tom the more I wished to see him well off in business or with a job. I got so I could not stand his coming to the house and asking me to sit while he recited. I began to dread his presence in the house as if his figure reminded me of my part in the mock play that his life was, and the prominence that my house and attention played.

One night I became desperate. "That book is destroying you, Tom. Why don't you give this up for awhile?"

He looked at me curiously without a word. He recited several pages and left early that evening.

Tom did not come to the house again. I guess it got so that Tom could not stand me any more than his uncle and parents. When he quit coming I felt bad. I knew he would never abandon his ambition. I was equally sure that Tom would never rank with the great Shakespearean actors, but I could not forget his simple persistence.

One day, years later, I saw him on the Piedmont car at Fourteenth and Broadway. He was sitting with his head buried in a book and I was sure it was a copy of Shakespeare's. For a moment he looked up and stared at me as if I were a stranger. Then his face broke into a smile and he raised his hand. I waved back eagerly.

"How are you, Tom?" I shouted.

He waved his hand politely again but did not get off, and the car started up Broadway.

Acknowledgments

Continued from page ii.

Doubleday: "Hamlet" by Yevgeny Vinokurov, translated by Daniel Weissbort, from *20th Century Russian Poetry,* selected by Yevgeny Yevtushenko. Copyright © 1993 by Doubleday, a division of Bantam Doubleday Dell Publishing Group, Inc. Used by permission of Doubleday, a division of Bantam Doubleday Dell Publishing Group, Inc.

Asian American Studies Center, UCLA : "Japanese Hamlet," from *The Chauvinist and Other Stories* by Toshio Mori. Copyright © 1979 by Asian American Studies Center, UCLA. Reprinted by permission of Asian American Studies Center, UCLA.